the natural
gardener

To Mum and Dad, whose philosophy has
always been: Don't say no to anything and
never be afraid to tread your own path.

This book is published to accompany the television series
entitled *The Flying Gardener,* which is shown on
BBC Television.

Series Producer (Flying Gardener series 1, 2 and Winter Flying
Gardener): Kathy Myers
Executive Producer: Owen Gay
Series Producer series 4: Gill Tierney
Executive Producer: Paul Wooding

Published by BBC Worldwide Limited, Woodlands,
80 Wood Lane, London W12 0TT

ISBN 0563 48804 2

Commissioning Editor: Vivien Bowler
Project Editor: Helena Caldon
Editor: Andi Clevely
Book Designer: Kathryn Gammon
Picture Researcher: Susannah Parker
Production Controller: Kenneth McKay
Jacket Art Direction: Pene Parker

Set in Swiss 721
Printed and bound in Italy by LEGO Spa
Colour separations by Radstock Reproductions,
Midsomer Norton

the natural
gardener
lessons from the landscape

chris
beardshaw

contents

understanding

To become a natural gardener, you have to plan and plant in sympathy with the land and landscape as it is. If you understand the soil and climate conditions in your garden; then you can choose the most suitable plants for your surroundings, and echo the surrounding natural landscape.

your environment

A garden is a combination of many ingredients. Its overall style and design, for example, can have infinite variations, depending on the gardener's taste and the materials used.

Then there are the plants. You might think at first that the same unlimited choice is open to you, whatever your plans – but to get the best from the plants you choose, it is essential to recognize that each has evolved to thrive in a specific set of conditions. To use any plant in your garden successfully, you need to provide it with a site that mimics its preferred surroundings in the wild.

A good gardener learns to read the garden's character and its unique conditions, which may vary from one end of the site to another. You can, of course, try to change the conditions that nature has bestowed upon you, although the whole concept of altering the environment is the antithesis of natural gardening, which is the art of working with the existing surroundings. To become a natural gardener, it's vital that you plan and plant in sympathy with the land and landscape as it is.

In order to establish the personality of your site, it is not enough to take a fleeting glance at the garden from the comfort of the house. No matter how wild or cultivated your plot, you must go outdoors to come to know and understand your garden. Your aim should be to analyse its character in order to recognize which of the natural landscapes you can learn from and imitate.

Within this analysis there are five main criteria – soil, light, water, wind and temperature – and you will need to understand their impact on the garden before you can be fully aware of the environmental conditions nature has given you. Any fear or trembling you might feel at the prospect of the scientific depth and dreary investigation involved in getting to grips with these criteria is unfounded: the analysis of your garden requires only common sense and a little guidance.

The reward for this preliminary effort will be thriving plants, growing in conditions that perfectly fit their needs. It is true that a plant in the wrong place will often survive, but that is not enough. The natural gardener wants every plant to positively flourish, growing to fulfil its maximum potential with the minimum of fuss, and it can only do this in its favourite environment.

soil

To many gardeners soil is something so mundane that it is frequently overlooked. Worse, it is often abused and neglected, and yet we expect it to provide nourishment and a stable foundation for the plants we choose with such care.

Determining your soil type and understanding its character is key to choosing plants which will thrive in their preferred conditions.

In order to understand soil we must first look at what it is. All soil is essentially composed of three elements – small particles of rock, organic matter and moisture. These three are combined in varying proportions to make up different kinds of soil, and each element plays a fundamental part in defining the soil's character.

The base rock from which the soil is formed is its primary inorganic ingredient, and the size of the mineral particles within the soil structure depends on the type of rock from which they are made. Chalk, for example, which is soft and easily broken, produces a soil containing large particles of rock, whereas granite, which is very hard, is eroded into much smaller fragments.

This mineral content is combined with organic matter, supplied in the form of dead and decaying plant or animal material. This is an essential ingredient for healthy plant growth, because organic matter contains all the nutrients that are broken down and used by plants for food. It also works physically as a sponge, absorbing moisture as this passes through the soil, holding it in suspension and making it available for plants to absorb through their roots.

Rainfall is the principle source of moisture for plants, but the amount of this the ground normally receives and stores up for future use by plants varies from one garden to another. Whether your soil can hold huge amounts of water or dries out quickly after a shower will often be the deciding factor between creating a dryish meadow or a wetland garden of moisture-loving plants.

Since plants have evolved and adapted to thrive in the very different soil types these three ingredients have combined to produce, you can see that it is essential to first assess the kind of soil you have before selecting plants for your plot. You only need about five minutes to gather the basic information about your soil. But they could be the most important five minutes in the life of the garden.

sandy soil

description Does not stay in a ball but crumbles away easily. It feels gritty between finger and thumb, looks fine and granular in texture, and is easy to dig.

landscape equivalent Coastal soils and dunes.

properties This is a very free-draining soil with little organic matter, so it has limited ability to retain water. Its light structure means it is easy to work, and warms up quickly in spring.

clay soil

description Easily rolled into a firm ball whose surface can be polished. It has a smooth, almost slimy texture between your fingers, looks sticky with clods, and may smell of rotten eggs.

landscape equivalent River valleys.

properties Clay is the opposite to sand, very slow to drain and susceptible to puddling after heavy rain. It is usually very fertile but very dense, so it is slow to warm up and to cool.

chalky soil

description Will not stay in a ball. It feels rough and gritty, with obvious pieces of chalk or flints, and is often very pale in colour.

landscape equivalent Chalk meadow.

properties This is usually a moderately fertile, shallow soil, with large particles of rock that make it very free-draining, so it is susceptible to drying out.

loamy soil

description This will mould into a ball, but breaks into pieces easily. It feels soft and slightly spongy between your fingers, and looks dark brown, often with obvious pieces of organic matter.

landscape equivalent Farmland, fertile plains.

properties Really the perfect soil and high in nutrients, this contains enough organic matter to allow it to retain moisture, but with good drainage it does not become waterlogged.

peaty soil

description Crumbles when you roll it or squeeze it into a ball. Very soft and spongy, it is black or very dark brown and may smell sour.

landscape equivalent Peat bog.

properties Peat soil is wet and acidic but high in nutrients, allowing it to support excellent plant growth.

Take a handful of moist soil and do three things. First, try to squeeze it into a firm ball, and then smear a smaller sample between your thumb and finger. Finally, study it carefully, noting its structure, texture, colour and smell. Armed with this information you should be able to identify your soil from a simple set of typical characteristics.

In a gardening context, each soil type has particular qualities that make it more suitable for some plants than for others. It is not simply a case of any one type being better for plant growth in general, but that certain plants have evolved natural adaptations to a particular soil's qualities or defects. The more information you have about your soil, the more power you have to choose the appropriate plants.

Each of these soil types is associated with a different pH, or level of acidity. A soil's pH is another of those examples of scientific jargon that intimidate many gardeners, but there is little mystery about it. Soils can be acid (sour), alkaline (limy) or somewhere in between, and the level of acidity is measured on what is called the pH scale. Knowing your soil's pH is essential for choosing the right plants for the site.

As a rough guide, clay and peat soils are acidic, chalky soil is alkaline, and sandy and loamy soils tend to be neutral (neither acid nor alkaline). You can check this by observing key plants growing naturally in your immediate environment, as many only really thrive in soils of a particular pH level. If you can see an abundance of healthy birch (*Betula*), foxglove (*Digitalis*), heather (*Erica*, *Calluna* or *Daboecia*), rhododendrons and camellias, you are almost certainly in an area of acidic soil. If, on the other hand, there are plenty of beech (*Fagus*) and ash (*Fraxinus*) trees, ceanothus, rosemary, rock roses (*Helianthemum*), cowslips, scabious and clematis, the soil is likely to be alkaline.

Since some plants are very fussy about the acidity or alkalinity of the soil and others can grow satisfactorily in both conditions, it is best to confirm your diagnosis by carrying out a pH test. Special soil-testing kits for this purpose are inexpensive, simple to use and readily available from garden centres. All you need to do is mix a little earth from your plot with some water and the testing powder, match the colour that emerges in the solution against a shade chart, and read off the corresponding pH number. This will be somewhere in the region of 1 to 14 – neutral is 6 to 8, results below 6 are acidic and those above 8 are increasingly alkaline.

The soil's acidity affects growth by regulating the nutrients available to plants. It is worth pausing at this stage to consider these nutrients, to understand their composition and the reasons why we add them to improve natural fertility and aid plant growth.

All plant nutrients are taken up from the soil, dissolved in solution and absorbed through the roots. The main foods are known as macro-nutrients: nitrogen (N), which is vital for leaf and stem growth, phosphorus (P) for strong root production, and potassium (K), which helps develop flowers and fruit. Magnesium (Mg), calcium (Ca) and sulphur (S) are other elements that plants need in fairly large quantities. Micro-nutrients are equally important to plants but required in much smaller amounts, rather like vitamins in our diet – these include iron (Fe), zinc (Zn), boron (B), molybdenum (Mo) and chlorine (Cl).

On the majority of sites you will find that only nitrogen, phosphorus and potassium need to be added, since most plant problems are caused by a lack of one of these three nutrients. Nitrogen deficiency, for example, causes reduced growth and yellowing of leaves, low potassium levels lead to leaf discoloration, and insufficient phosphorus (the least common deficiency) results in slow growth and dull foliage. Whatever your soil type, it is a good idea to incorporate a fertilizer containing N, P and K at some stage. This does not betray the principle of natural gardening, because we are only adding this food to encourage our new plants to thrive, without actually altering the natural state of the soil.

You can add the necessary nutrients quickly and easily by using chemical fertilizers, but these concentrated feeds lack the structural bulk provided by organic materials such as rotted manure or mushroom compost. Although these may have a proportionally lower nutrient content compared with chemical fertilizers, their bulky composition improves the structure of the soil, providing the perfect conditions for beneficial micro-organisms, good water absorption and healthy growth.

water

Much of the rain reaching the surface of the soil is lost back to the atmosphere by evaporation. The water that does penetrate the soil is stored there in the particles of organic matter, which act like tiny sponges, or is suspended in capillary pores, the fine empty spaces between the soil fragments.

Water can only be held in pores that are less than 0.1mm (⁴⁄₁₀₀₀in) diameter – anything larger is filled with air, which is also essential for plant growth and an ingredient of well-structured soil. The size and holding capacity of these pores varies according to the soil type. Clay soils have the finest particles, separated by huge numbers of very small pores, so these can store the greatest amount of water, whereas sandy soils have large capillary pores between their bigger particles, making them less able to retain water and more free-draining.

Plants absorb the water stored in the soil through fine hairs on their roots, and once water is inside the plant it performs three functions: it is essential for photosynthesis, the plant's basic living process (see Light); it acts as a means of transport to move nutrients around within the plant; and it maintains turgidity in the stems, keeping them upright and self-supporting. A constant supply of water is necessary to maintain growth – if the water supply decreases, plant functions slow down, stomata (tiny breathing holes) on the leaves close to reduce transpiration, and if no more water is available the plant will wilt and may eventually die.

In arid areas where the water supply is naturally sparse, native plants have developed adaptations that allow them to thrive with minimal amounts of water. Their leaves may have special characteristics such as hairs, spines or sticky coatings that help to reduce the rate of transpiration taking place – examples include thistles, cacti and many sticky-leaved cistus. The leaves of plants like lavender and rosemary have evolved with such a small surface area that water

loss is reduced, while others such as sedums and sempervivums have expanded to form their own water storage units within the stems and leaves.

For plants without these adaptations we may occasionally have to resort to manual watering. This is not desirable as a general practice, since the aim of natural gardening is to provide plants with the most favourable conditions so that they can grow happily without too much interference from the gardener, but a new plant may need to be watered regularly during its first season if rainfall is insufficient. Even where the rainfall level is adequate, walls or buildings can shade plants and restrict the amount of water reaching them. When you do water, remember that little and often only dampens the top of the soil, encouraging plants to keep their roots close to the surface, whereas drenching the ground less frequently encourages them to put down deep stable roots.

from left to right Plants such as thistles, lavender and echevaria have adapted to survive in hot, dry conditions. They reduce the amount of water lost through transpiration by having spines, thin leaves with a small surface area or expanded leaves which store water.

light

Gardeners talk a lot about aspect – the way a garden faces – which influences the amount of light it receives. Knowing the aspect of your garden is one of the fundamental pieces of information that you need when assessing its qualities, but this is not quite as simple as it sounds.

Even the smallest garden will have areas with different aspects. Within a generally south-facing plot, for example, there will also be boundaries that face north, so that they are sheltered from much of the daily sun. There might be corners that bask in the first few hours of morning light, but are shadowed by

from left to right Plants can also adapt themselves to make the most of the sunlight afforded to them. In shady areas plants can thrive by maximizing the surface area of their leaves to absorb the sunlight needed for photosynthesis, or reduce it by having variegated leaves in order to survive in stronger light levels.

buildings for the rest of the day, while trees can cast deep shade almost anywhere within a sunny garden.

Since light is essential for all plant growth, you need to be aware of its quantity and quality in your plot. A weekend spent observing your garden – watching where the sunlight falls, and noting its duration and intensity – can provide you with vital information that will help when you come to choose the plants most likely to thrive there.

Seasonal and regional differences must always be taken into account. Light levels in summer, for example, can be much higher in an open meadow garden but lower in a woodland, once deciduous trees are covered in leaves. Spring travels quite slowly, and in Britain can arrive up to one month later in gardens 100 miles further north. Gardeners in Scotland experience summer much later than those in Kent, and gardens there will always remain slightly cooler than their southern counterparts.

We know from experience that plants need light, but what do they use it for? Sunlight falls on their leaves, and these – whether they are needles or tendrils – are the manufacturing centres for the plant, where the vital process of photsynthesis produces energy. Each leaf contains green pigment called chlorophyll, which absorbs the sunlight as fuel during the day in order to convert water and carbon dioxide from the atmosphere into carbohydrates. Oxygen is released into the air as a by-product. Some of this is re-absorbed through the leaves as the plant breaks down the carbohydrates to produce energy, a process called respiration.

Generally leaves need to expose a large surface area to maximize the absorption of essential light, something that is particularly noticeable in plants accustomed to meagre light levels, such as those species that exist in the shade under a forest canopy. Plants that have not adapted in this way respond to shade by stretching towards the available light source, often producing leaves mainly on the sunniest side of the plant. In the worst cases, the plant becomes etiolated, with weak leggy stems and poor pale growth, and more prone to diseases.

At the other extreme, a plant that develops brown scorch marks on the edges of new foliage is probably growing in conditions that are too bright, when it would prefer some dappled shade. Plant varieties that have foliage variegated with yellow or white stripes or bronzy undertones can thrive in stronger light levels because each leaf has a smaller area of green surface available for photosynthesis, and these plants usually react to shade by turning almost completely green.

wind

The water available to plants can be inadequate for a number of reasons. Strong sunshine has a drying effect, evaporating moisture from plants and the surrounding earth, but high winds can desiccate a garden as effectively as the hottest summer day.

Perhaps surprisingly, this is often a problem that affects built-up areas much more acutely than rural gardens. Barriers such as buildings and walls create solid masses that are impermeable to wind, which has to find an alternative route around the obstruction, channelling it into turbulent eddies and wind tunnels. So if you try to limit the impact of high winds by erecting barriers, a solid boundary such as a fence or wall erected around a garden for protection may only achieve the opposite, by forcing the wind over the structure and increasing its potential to damage plants. It is best to use instead a more permeable boundary such as a hedge or shelter-belt of trees to filter the wind, limiting its speed and considerably reducing the problem.

Plants found in nature's wildest places, where there is no available protection from the wind, have evolved natural adaptations that allow them to survive uninjured. The most evident of these is reduced size, and plants such as alpines that grow on rock faces regularly blasted with wind, for example, have developed low mound-forming shapes, barely raising their heads above the cracks in the rock. Many alpines also have much deeper roots, which can tap lower levels of water to compensate for that lost from their leaves by the wind's drying effect.

temperature

You may think at first that the temperature of your site is determined only by the amount of available sunshine, a factor over which we have no influence – apart, perhaps, from limiting any shade in the garden. There is another important environmental influence, however, which can radically change the temperature of your plot and over which we do have some control, and that is frost.

The air on a cold morning can bring frost rather like flowing water, travelling downhill until it settles on the lower levels at the base of hills and in dips in the ground. If your plot is low-lying or near the bottom of a slope, the downward movement of the heavy cold air will be interrupted, causing it to linger around any solid objects, in this case your house.

The adjacent garden will have a microclimate that is cooler than the surrounding area, and this will inevitably influence your plant selection. You can modify the impact of frost to some degree by deflecting the cooling air with a shelter-belt of hardy plants and trees, which will absorb and redirect the air flow in much the same way as it can shield a windy site.

Even with the protection of a shelter-belt, though, it is worth avoiding those plants that are most vulnerable to cold blasts of frost. These include early-flowering fruits such as apples, cherries and pears, as well as many summer annuals and tender perennials, although these will usually be safe if you plant them out two or three weeks later than you would in more sheltered spots.

Having established all the information you need about your soil type and its pH level, together with the aspect and exposure of the garden, you should have a more intimate understanding of the growing conditions available to you, and you can start choosing suitable plants that are in tune with the garden's character. To guide you in your selection, we need to look at the different kinds of natural landscape you can mimic in the garden to ensure the plants are growing in the surroundings they enjoy most.

Consider the climate and microclimate in your garden before selecting your plants. Tender species may not survive a frost, but other hardier plants, such as these silver birches, can look wonderfully dramatic in a covering of frost.

the natural

The physical conditions of the natural rock garden can vary considerably, from the solid bare rock-faces of immovable mountains to unstable gravel slopes, rock ledges, smooth outcrops and level pavements – but there are plants that will endure all of these positions.

rock garden

origins

of the natural rock garden

Someone once described mountains as empty places where no plants grow, and it is true that the continuous cover of vegetation we take for granted at lower levels thins out dramatically as you climb upwards. Above the tree line, at heights where the inhospitable environment prevents woodland from establishing, rocks appear at the surface and the plant cover peters out.

As anyone familiar with the conditions that prevail on mountains and cliff tops will agree, this is not a landscape in which we might reasonably expect to find plants in abundance, billowing one over another, but rather a patchy and incomplete plant cover settling and colonizing the gaps and cracks between bare rocks. Perhaps the most astonishing thing about these plants is their diversity, caused by the fact that what might appear at first sight to be a uniform barren region in fact includes a range of different habitats. The physical conditions of the natural rock garden can vary considerably, from the solid bare rock-faces of immovable mountains to unstable gravel slopes, rock ledges, smooth outcrops and level pavements, and even small areas of lush, springy meadow, and there are plants for every one of these positions.

What all these plants and planting sites have in common are the geological features that underlie them. Cliffs, limestone pavements and mountain peaks are all features made up of protruding rocks that are hard enough to resist erosion. Most are very old and date from the great age of earth-building hundreds of millions of years ago. Some were laid down at the bottom of long-vanished seas and then squeezed and consolidated into tough limestones, marbles and slates. Others were boiled, baked and blended in the hearts of volcanoes before being left to cool as lavas and granites harder than concrete.

Their incredible resistance to the elements results in slowing the process of weathering, which can take many thousands of years to make the slightest impact, unlike softer rocks that are quickly shattered and worn down by wind, frost and rain into smaller fragments. The release of mineral particles as a result of this rock erosion is an essential stage in the development of soil, and the extremely slow weathering of hard volcanic rocks causes soils in these regions to develop painfully slowly. Even when particles do break away from the parent rock, they are frequently blown away by high wind or washed downhill by torrential rain, ending up in the fertile soils of the valleys and lowlands. Any plant that wants to thrive in these unfriendly regions must be able to grow in just a handful of unpromising soil tucked away in crevices and cracks in the rock.

The soil that does form here and there tends to be well-supplied with mineral nutrients but low in organic material, for the simple reason that there are relatively few plants to die and add their decomposed remains to enrich the growing environment. Because of this the soils tend to be unstable, their loose grains ever shifting under the influence of water and wind, except where lodged in deep crevices or bound together by plant roots. Occasionally whole areas of unstable rock, undermined by erosion or disturbed by severe weather, will collapse and shift tons of rock fragments downhill, where they settle in large piles of debris at the foot of cliffs. This process produces loose, free-draining scree, a habitat that discourages most plants but which has its own specialized flora, as we shall see.

I am always amazed that some plants can thrive in such apparently harsh conditions as these – exposed to all the elements and with little protection.

Rugged and dramatic landscapes have been an inspiration for gardeners since as early as the eighteenth century.

The challenges don't stop there. The altitude associated with so many of these landscapes has an adverse effect on the prevailing temperature, which tends to fall by 0.5°C for every 100m (0.9°F/328ft) as you climb. That is just the average air temperature, but exposure leads to harsh extremes, and the ground may be baked by summer sunlight, especially in the absence of shade from woody vegetation and on slopes at right angles to the sun's rays, while in winter the area can be bitten by frost or buried under several feet of snow. Throw in gales, the associated wind chill and the inevitable drying of foliage, and you will agree that things do not look promising for plants. Conditions are even worse during the winter months when the typically high and concentrated rainfall washes not only soil particles but also vital nutrients down towards the valleys.

Of course, it is not all bad news, otherwise no plants could grow there at all. The generally hostile conditions ensure that rock garden plants suffer little or no competition from others. The pockets of available soil and shelter among precipitous rock faces and shifting gravelly slopes are usually tiny, with just enough room for a single plant adapted to exploit the meagre resources. The only chance another plant has of moving in during the short, favourable growing season is often when the original dies or moves on downhill. Rock garden communities are continually changing under the influence of hard weather, running

Scrambling up the last few feet of a hill, cliff or mountain summit is for me one of the most emotionally uplifting and rewarding experiences to be had in the landscape. As I stand thousands of feet above the average domestic garden, shrouded in wisps of mist and surveying a scene of barren rock, the views are always spectacular and the solitude is refreshing.

It's easy to feel there is little in these landscapes to interest a gardener. The only obvious plants are lichens, mosses and a scattering of fine grasses, all flattened by the wind. However, this is home to some of the most remarkable survival experts, the natural rock garden plants that may not be immediately obvious because they are often minute and hide themselves away, not from people, but from the weather.

Most of us only head for the hills when it is pleasant enough for a stroll, but anyone who has spent time there will know the weather can change quickly from placid to vicious. Just a few hours in a snowstorm on Snowdon will make you appreciate exactly what these plants have to put up with. They are equipped to survive in the toughest conditions you offer them in the garden.

water and shifting rocks, with some plants being uprooted and carried down to settle once more on a rock ledge, leaving the higher nooks and crannies for newcomers.

Some of the soils in mountain regions are very acid, partly because the rocks from which they are formed were acid in the first place and also because many of the earliest and most capable plants to colonize bare habitats are mosses. As these decay, their remains increase the acidity and peatiness of the soils, which limits the range of species that can grow there. And, of course, growing in a loose bed of rock fragments or hanging off a cliff face does ensure fantastic drainage and most rock plants have evolved to cope with this feature of high, bare ground. Water rushes downhill everywhere in the uplands under the influence of gravity, and the heaviest rainfall soon vanishes through the porous granular rock fragments.

But, as any gardener knows, the ground under a rock stays moist for longer than elsewhere, so most mountain habitats manage to combine fast drainage of surplus water with conservation of enough moisture to support growth. This is a unique characteristic that allows tough rock garden plants to survive in an otherwise hostile environment, and is a feature you need to find or imitate when creating your own natural rock garden.

identifying
the potential rock garden

You might think this is the most obvious of all natural environments to identify, and despair because you cannot look out of your window at craggy beds of weathered granite. You certainly will not want to rebuild the Matterhorn, and anyway it is quite difficult to create the illusion of a mountain chain in a back garden, even in miniature. But although the raw rock may be missing from the domestic garden, the harsh and barren conditions of its natural counterpart are not. The exposure of Snowdonian rock formations and the typical domestic garden are not as far apart as you might think, and the windswept environment of a contemporary roof garden or terrace, for example, can share many of the inhospitable qualities of a craggy mountain top.

In fact, virtually every garden I have visited has included a site where few plants grow happily or easily because of its challenging nature. It might be an old heap of rubble, an exposed wall, a bare gravel area or a stony, sun-baked corner – to me, these are missed opportunities to cultivate a stunning range of plants that would prefer those spartan conditions to more fertile spots in the garden. We all have one or more of these barren patches, and that is precisely why the rock garden should be in every garden landscape and its plants, the mountain goats of the horticultural world, part of every gardener's repertoire.

Perhaps you have never paused to appreciate some of these tiny plants that spend their lives hiding precariously under rocks. It was the Victorians who, in their ceaseless quest for novelty, ventured furthest into the Alps of central Europe to harvest these curious little gems, bringing them back to replant in huge rock gardens that developed into replicas of whole mountain ranges to house their expanding collections. They referred to these rock garden plants as 'alpines', although this term strictly refers to those species that come from the highest cold altitudes where the growing season is unbelievably short. In fact rock garden plants can be found from sea cliffs to mountain tops all round the globe, anywhere that the underlying rock is exposed nakedly at the surface.

Other conditions need to be present too, but luckily these are seldom hard to find and may even be an existing problem, if gardeners' typical complaints are anything to go by. Shallow soils of low fertility, an exposed and windswept site away from overhanging trees (shelter, which is valuable, is quite a different quality from overhead shade, which can be lethal to plants used to the open sky), stony ground that drains freely but stays moist in drought, and little competition from other plants, perhaps because nothing much grows there anyway – if the site offers most of these qualities, you can hardly go wrong. Already you have managed to match the most important features of the natural rock garden.

Don't despair if your conditions seem less than ideal. There are in truth as many different habitats for rock plants as there are for any other plant group, and there is easily as much diversity among the plants themselves. Walking through the kind of wild landscape inhabited by rock plants really makes you appreciate just how varied their surroundings can be: from wholly sun-lit cliffs and slopes to deep crevices and overhung ledges buried in the dense shade of nearby rocks, from windswept peaks and steep arid screes to sheltered boulders and damp patches in dips and hollows. All the essential conditions are present, even if superficially the sites differ wildly.

When a gardener understands his or her conditions, a rock garden can become a riot of colour and an otherwise hard landscape can be softened by planting.

Let's start with the rocks themselves. It is easy to get technical at this point, because there are many kinds with a different mineral make-up depending on their origin, and their typical flora can reflect this closely. In Britain, for example, there are the limestones and chalks of North Yorkshire and the South Downs cliffs. These are porous, absorbing and holding water readily, and break down eventually to produce a calcium-rich (alkaline) soil that is ideally suited to maidenhair fern (*Adiantum capillus-veneris*) and reflexed stonecrop (*Sedum reflexum*). The granites, slates and schists of the Snowdonia and Dartmoor National Parks are dense, making them impermeable to water – these weather slowly and break down to create an acid soil that is colonised by plants like the Highland saxifrage (*Saxifraga rivularis*) and mossy cyphel (*Minuartia sedoides*).

In many gardens the structural work will already be in place and you will have little choice over the type of rock to be used. This need not matter because you can mix up a gritty universal compost to fill the gaps in between, and your plants should flourish in this, whatever their natural preferences. If you are starting from scratch, sourcing the rocks locally is the best solution aesthetically because they will blend the garden into the surrounding landscape, and any minerals they release as they weather should not conflict with the existing garden soil, which makes plant selection easy.

The dark, craggy outcrops and pavements of natural stone can easily be translated into miniature gardens.

Do not simply dot the rocks here and there on a mound of soil, in the contrived, erratic and very unnatural rockery style of the 1970s. The natural rock garden should be closer to the Victorian ideal. This style avoided round rocks and thin slabs placed on the surface, concentrating instead on angular stones placed with their broadest side on the ground and at least half buried in the soil, so that they protruded in natural layers or beds to form terraces, plateaux and outcrops. This style created the crevices and ledges, some sunny and others shaded, that plants would naturally choose to grow in.

They will need some kind of rooting medium, apart from rubble and stone fragments. Although plants generally have different moisture requirements, the evolutionary history of rock species has produced plants that conserve moisture or make maximum use of limited or erratic supplies, so it stands to reason that a poorly drained soil is unsuitable. Even those plants that prefer a consistent supply of moisture require free drainage – no rock plant likes sitting with its feet in the water! In the garden you can ensure good soil drainage by incorporating plenty of fine grit or by raising the level of the ground with a special soil mixture. I use a blend of equal parts garden compost, grit and loam for rock and scree plants, while for those living in cracks and crevices you can usually replace the grit with leaf mould to help conserve a little more moisture.

Many gardeners choose alpine plants to provide the perfect carpet around the base of trees and shrubs.

Pack these mixtures in planting nooks and cracks, or spread them in a layer up to 30cm (12in) deep over a bed of coarse stones and aggregate, before adding the rocks to achieve the final effect.

Alpines are so versatile that they allow you to seek out existing habitats within the present structure of the garden that still offer the conditions suitable for the rock plants. Gaps in steps and crevices in walls are as effective as nooks and crannies between large boulders for a great number of plants that can transform these normally bare areas into living features. The edges and joints of patio stones offer good drainage, a cool moist root run as well as the sun-warmed surroundings favoured by natural pavement plants, like tiny silenes and campanulas. The borders of gravel paths are natural screes, with a deep

■ The best rock gardens are made from hard rocks that do not break or shatter easily after frost – these include slate, granite and some of the tougher limestones. Whichever you choose, remember to select plants that would naturally grow on that type of rock.

■ Although it can be expensive and difficult to find, tufa is a porous alkaline rock that is perfect for alpine gardens and can be carved to make small planting pockets for tiny species. Just one or two choice pieces can make a superb alpine container.

■ If possible, visit a stone-yard or quarry to find and buy your rocks. It can be far more economical and you can choose attractive pieces of different sizes, but make sure they are small enough to handle if you are building the rock garden yourself.

stony layer in which plants can root and provide some of the best drainage in the whole garden.

And remember that even tough alpine plants are not indestructible. When you are only 2cm (¾in) high the microclimate can change even more rapidly than it does in a rambling garden, and the protection offered by a rock the size, say, of a dinner plate might mean the difference between life and death. Examine carefully the amount of sun a location gets, its moisture levels, depth of soil and exposure to wind, and treat every tiny crack and crevice as an individual garden that might suit a particular species. When building up your rock garden you have an advantage over nature, because you can create exactly the right conditions for the plants you wish to grow.

plants
of the natural rock garden

Every rock garden species employs a combination of tactics to ensure its survival, but this specialization means that each one requires a specific set of growing conditions. The key to understanding where plants should be positioned in the garden can be found by studying both the type of environment in which each is found and the structure of the plant itself.

Most members of the plant kingdom have spent millennia evolving methods of ensuring that they can thrust their heads towards the sun, from which they derive the energy to allow them to compete energetically for light, water and space. Generations of rock plants have taken a different approach, however, choosing instead to hang precariously on barren rock faces, where the best chance of survival lay not in competing with other plants but literally in keeping their heads down to avoid physical damage. It is no surprise, then, that they are all small in stature.

Their other physical adaptations vary according to the kind of surroundings in which they are typically found, but most species can be regarded as belonging to one or other of two broad habitat types.

rock and scree plants

These plants live in the most hostile kind of rock garden environment, nestling among blocks of ageing and immovable rock or the smaller loose fragments that make up a scree bed. There they are at the mercy of the weather, and so tend to be smaller in overall size to reduce the possibility of injury from high winds. In addition the size of their leaves is often massively reduced to limit the amount of water lost from the surface by evaporation in the wind. A perfect example is wild thyme (*Thymus serpyllum*), with intensely aromatic 4mm (⅛in) leaves and pink summer flowers on wiry shrubs sometimes less than 5cm (2in) high. You can plant this in groups to imitate the attractive alpine lawns often

found half-way up a mountain-side, carpeting a ledge where precious leaf-litter and moisture have been trapped.

Alternatively a plant may develop a soft fuzz of hairs on its leaf surfaces, a cunning adaptation to prevent water loss in high winds. Most of this potentially harmful evaporation occurs on the underside of the leaves, and a plant such as the delicate and charming white-flowered mountain avens (*Dryas octopetala*) may be so downy or 'tomentose' that the lower leaf surfaces appear greyish-white in colour. This is a real Arctic survivor – not only is it a prostrate miniature plant, just 8–10cm (3–4in) high, with hairy defences below, but the top side of its small oak-like leaves is protected with a glossy, waxy coating to prevent water loss and reflect sunshine, so avoiding injury from intense ultraviolet light. Like many rock garden plants, it flowers in late spring and early summer, in that brief interlude between melting snow and burning summer sunlight.

In addition to reducing their leaves to a safe size, plants that are used to living in exposed positions often grow in tight, compact cushions or spreading mats that can look almost moss-like. Wild thyme and mountain avens are both typical carpeting species, but mossy saxifrage (*Saxifraga hypnoides*) and moss campion (*Silene acaulis*) are even more extreme, forming dense, tangled mats that act like blankets, protecting the crown of the plant from cold weather. The individual leaves are so small and tightly packed that they are almost impossible to distinguish. As a further survival technique, the short leafy stems break off easily in high winds, which carry them to new sites where they root almost straight away.

Some plants rely on producing leaves that flatten themselves against the surface of the rock. Mountain everlasting or cat's foot (*Antennaria dioica*), for example, produces a perfect star-shaped rosette of foliage, covered in white hairs underneath and forming a 5cm (2in) low profile that reduces the possibility of wind damage while benefiting from the radiant heat of the rock when it is warmed by the sun. Only when its dense woolly clusters of pink flowers spring up in early June does it raise its head to the daring height of about 20cm (8in).

Summers can be dry among the mountain tops and sun-baked boulders, and to cope with the resulting lack of readily-available soil moisture some species store water in expanded cells in the leaf and stem, rather like desert cacti and succulents that have learned to save the surplus for a rainless day. The compact bright yellow-flowered roseroot (*Rhodiola rosea*) and its close cousin, the tiny hairy stonecrop (*Sedum villosum*) both have thick fleshy leaves, many of them overlapping to partially shade each other, and thrive in full sun among rocks where there is little or no soil.

Such cunning adaptations enable the plants to flourish unscathed in barren exposed positions. They are perennials – like most species from these habitats where the short growing season mitigates against annuals, which need more time to complete their cycle from germination to self-seeding – and all are from necessity remarkably hardy, easily able to tolerate subzero temperatures. However, during winter they all rely on a dusting of snow to help them through the most savage season of the year. The snow layer acts like a duvet, under which they can lie relatively dry, dormant and safe from the raging elements outside.

These native British plants are just some of nature's solutions to coping with the kind of hostile environment offered by bare mountainsides and tops. One other remarkable quality about them all is that, although wild, they are so delicate (only in appearance, though!) and attractive that they merit inclusion in the garden, and easily rival the 'improved' products of plant breeders. If you add to them other plants selected from the extensive range of exotics found growing all round the globe, the range of choice is bewildering, but irresistible. All you need remember to do is check the rock and habitat type each prefers.

A huge proportion of rock plants seem to have white, soft pink or light yellow blooms, and you might expect to struggle to find a flamboyant blast of colour to

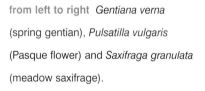

from left to right *Gentiana verna* (spring gentian), *Pulsatilla vulgaris* (Pasque flower) and *Saxifraga granulata* (meadow saxifrage).

light up your rock garden. But you would be mistaken, for the most intensely blue species of the whole plant world is a true rock plant found on limestone and other alkaline soils in most of the European mountains. The spring gentian (*Gentiana verna*) may only grow 4–5cm (1½–2in) tall, but you can see its vivid blooms from the other side of the garden, especially if you grow the more vigorous form *G. v. subsp. balcanica* (syn. 'Angulosa'), which has larger, brilliant cobalt flowers.

For a sprinkling of more delicate blue with a hint of lilac, try the alpine pincushion (*Scabiosa lucida*) a dainty scabious from central Europe. This is a wonderful clump-forming plant that looks almost too fragile to withstand the high alpine blasts, with tufts of silvery-green leaves and thin wiry flower stalks about 20cm (8in) high, which you can cut for long-lasting colour in vases indoors, and attractive seedheads. Another lime-lover like scabious and the spring gentian is the Pasque flower (*Pulsatilla vulgaris*), a feathery-leaved native of turfy alpine meadows and local areas of southern Britain that produces cup-shaped blooms in spring. Each flower has a yellow centre, although the petals can be any colour from pink through purple to red, and fades to leave a seedhead that is buried in a curious froth of silky hairs.

No alpine scheme would be complete without those most typical of mountain plants, the saxifrages. These form a huge and diverse family of over 400 species, mainly mat- or cushion-forming perennials with perfect white, pink or sometimes yellow single flowers waving cheerily on stiff stems above chubby mounds of packed foliage. *Saxifraga granulata*, the meadow saxifrage or fair maids of France, is widely available and, although a native of moister pastures, would not look out of place in an alpine meadow. One of the best for dry rocky places is *S. cebennensis*, a mossy white-flowered species from France that is often recommended for growing under glass in an alpine house to protect its tight hemispherical cushions from winter wetness. The way to ensure its survival outdoors is to plant it just as it grows in the wild, almost on its side among plenty of rocks and scree so that rainfall drains away quickly from its vulnerable crown.

Most rock garden saxifrages are evergreen or semi-evergreen, which helps relieve the starkness of bare rocks on a dull winter's day. For more evergreen ground cover, you could explore the huge races of sedums and sempervivums (stonecrops and houseleeks), usually mentioned in the same breath because they are both succulent members of the crassula family, with fleshy leaves and an ability to grow new plants from just a piece of a single leaf. They are low, spreading plants that can colonize large areas and survive the harshest conditions provided they have sun and good drainage, and their foliage is so

cuttings

well adapted to intense desiccation that they are the perfect choice for a sun-drenched roof garden or patio.

The plain common houseleek (*Sempervivum tectorum*) is perhaps best for the natural rock garden, but it is hard to resist the Central European cobweb houseleek (*S. arachnoideum*) whose red-tipped rosettes are trussed up elegantly in a network of fine white threads. The main plant of any houseleek dies after producing its thick stalk of starry midsummer flowers, leaving a ring of tiny offspring to grow on for the following year. There are also hundreds of hybrid houseleeks with subtly different flower or leaf colours. Some sedums, like the biting stonecrop (*Sedum acre*), can be weedy and invasive, but one of the choicest rock garden types is *S. lydium*, which forms tight mats of minute, red-tinged cylindrical leaves and dense heads of small white flowers in June.

You might be surprised to find shrubs and trees thriving in such extreme conditions, but there are a few diminutive forms of well-known lowland species that brave the bleak open zone above the natural tree line, keeping their heads well down from the searing wind. *Salix apoda*, for example, is a gnarled, almost prostrate dwarf willow from the Caucasus that slowly grows to about 45cm (18in) tall, a fraction of the height of more familiar willows. Most of the plants sold are the male form, which bears in spring 4cm (1½in) long silky grey-white catkins that turn golden-orange as they mature. Other choice miniature willows include *S. reticulata*, the net-leaved willow that grows wild in Scottish mountains and makes a mat of silvery-grey, textured oval leaves with golden candle-like catkins, and the dwarf willow (*S. herbacea*) with its creeping network of stems and round glossy foliage.

Any plant with Arctic in its common name might be assumed to be tough, and the Arctic or dwarf birch (*Betula nana*) lives up to its name, thriving in conditions of acid soil and semi-permanent snow and capable of surviving the worst your local climate can throw at it. It is the only real dwarf birch, seldom reaching 90cm (3ft) high but making a disproportionately huge impact twice a year, first when the dense mound of twiggy stems is covered with a spring flush of conspicuous golden-brown catkins, and again in autumn when the tiny rounded leaves turn rich gold or red before falling.

If you would rather have shrubs that bear more conventional flowers instead of catkins, you might prefer to plant *Hebe pinguifolia*, an upright or semi-prostrate New Zealand evergreen that can reach 90cm (3ft) tall, but is usually grown in one of its cultivated forms such as 'Pagei', just 30cm (12in) high. Its tiny oval leaves, somewhere between blue-green and silver-grey, are studded with masses of small, pure white flower heads all summer. Even smaller is the evergreen shrub with a big name, *Rhodothamnus chamaecistus*, which makes a dense 15–20cm (6–8in) mound of tiny, white-bristled leaves and clear pink bowl-shaped flowers. A native of Siberia and the Dolomites, it needs full sun on its foliage and a cool acid root-run beneath large rocks.

crack and crevice plants

Unlike the plants we have looked at so far, all of which are happy to revel all day in the sun, there are many that prefer the seclusion and cool shelter offered by depressions among the rocks. Such sites have the benefit of being tucked away from the worst gales and the drying effects of sunshine, and are often sufficiently recessed to allow soil particles to gather and catch the surface water as it trickles and percolates over impermeable rocks into every available crack and crevice. The result is the kind of habitat that is moist, shaded and sheltered, which sounds rather pleasant until you remember that it might be at a chilly altitude of more than 1,000m (3,280ft)!

Plants that thrive in these protected locations display fewer climatic adaptations in their foliage than their sun-loving cousins, although most tend to have large or abundant foliage in order to capture as much light as possible in their relatively shaded homes. Ferns such as the northern holly fern (*Polystichum lonchitis*) and the mountain parsley fern (*Cryptogramma crispa*) for example, have finely-cut leaves that, when taken in total, make up a large absorbent surface area. The alpine lady's mantle (*Alchemilla alpina*) from the mountains of Northern Europe also has a lush crop of rounded palmate leaves. They are more decorative than those of its more familiar border cousin *A. mollis*, but just as copious. It displays another survival technique called 'apomixis', which is the

from left to right *Betula nana* (dwarf birch), *Hebe pinguifolia* 'Pagei' (disk-leaved hebe) and *Viola riviniana* Purpurea Group (dog-violet).

ability to set seed without fertilization, a useful precaution in regions where pollination can be uncertain.

Some species keep their roots and crowns tucked safely in the shelter of the crevice, while thrusting long-stalked flowers into the open where they more easily attract passing insects that might aid pollination. The pretty purple-flowered common dog-violet (*Viola riviniana*) the closely related yellow mountain pansy *V. lutea*, and the leafy common wintergreen (*Pyrola minor*) all employ this tactic and the first you see of them as you scramble through the landscape is a cluster of nodding flowers emerging on 20–30cm (8–12in) stems from the most unlikely of crevices. Most spectacular of all is *Saxifraga cotyledon*, a native of high Scandinavian and Icelandic crevices, with secretive encrusted leaf rosettes that suddenly launch huge 60cm (2ft) plumes of tiny white flowers into the mid-summer sunshine.

Finally, there are a few wild rock plants that seem resigned to life being hard up among the mountains and have evolved ways of patiently sitting out the worst of the weather. Their usual method is to develop a tough storage rhizome that penetrates deep beneath the rocks where there is always enough water for life, allowing them to withstand extended periods of drought, whether in summer or while all around is frozen solid. Ferns are very adept at this, and the common moonwort (*Botrychium lunaria*) and the rusty back fern (*Asplenium ceterach*) are both capable in this way of allowing their normally lush foliage to die down in times of drought, and can remain dormant until sufficient moisture is available for growth to resume. Remarkably, they can wait for as long as three years.

Because they need to develop enough foliage to capture as much light as possible, garden forms of crevice plants have a reputation for being less glam-orous than their sun-loving cousins, but that is an unfair generalization. Some are certainly predominantly green and, as you might expect, high on the list of these are some choice ferns. Their strong searching roots allow them to perch in the tiniest of crannies, and they are an excellent choice for ledges, steps, walls and odd corners where they provide delightful splashes of embroidered greenery. One of the tiniest is wall rue (*Asplenium ruta-muraria*), a totally drought-resistant British native of dry limestone nooks and crannies, with little evergreen tufts of fan-shaped leaflets rarely more than 10cm (4in) long. The mountain fern, *Oreopteris limbosperma* (syn. *Thelypteris limbosperma*), is a striking contrast in size, its elegant 75cm (30in) fronds making a verdant back-drop to rocky screes.

A few members of the *Ranunculus* or buttercup family, one that you normally associate with damp lowland meadows and wetlands, can be found in high crevices and screes, where their comparatively large wide-awake flowers supply goblets of delicate colour in otherwise sombre surroundings. The lovely snow buttercup (*R. glacialis*) has 4cm (1½in) white blooms that fade softly to pink as they age, like those of *R. parnassiifolius* from the alpine heights. Further east, the Atlas Mountains provide *R. calandrinioides*, a fleshy-rooted species that dies right down in summer after its early spring flush of unbelievably beautiful white blooms.

For a real explosion of colour, you cannot better the primrose family, many members of which thrive happily among cool stones, either in full sun low down in the rock garden where moisture collects, or in partial shade in drier sites. One of the best European species for alkaline sites – you can even grow it on a heap of old mortar rubble – is *Primula marginata*, an almost evergreen primrose just 8cm (3in) high, with blue or lavender spring flowers on white powdered stems. A particularly floriferous species is *P. hirsuta* (syn. *P. rubra*), with numerous heads of clear pink flowers. It is rather happier in dry spots than the Caucasian *P. juliae*, which relishes pockets of leafy soil among the rocks. The species has rich magenta blooms, but is probably best known for its hybrids with the common wild primrose. These are the Wanda Group hybrids, which can be almost any shade of rose, deep red, violet and even yellow, and are all gorgeous.

Although it might be more familiar to you as a border perennial, the Welsh poppy (*Meconopsis cambrica*) is a true rock garden plant from the cliffs and hills of the Atlantic coastline. It is perhaps the easiest meconopsis to grow, so adaptable and good-tempered that some gardeners regard it as a weed. True, it does have a habit when happy of setting seed all over the garden, but for all that, it is a particular favourite of mine and I rather like its cheerfully informal habit and bright orange-yellow flowers. Sow it wherever there are cracks and crevices, and it will choose the best and thrive without further ado.

Most other kinds of meconopsis are rather fussy and can be difficult as well as too tall for most rock gardens. This includes the almost legendary Himalayan Blue poppy (*Meconopsis grandis*) whose stems of intensely blue flowers can reach a surprising 1.2m (4ft) high. It is really a woodland plant and is most likely to succeed in cool shade and leafy acid soils. If you really must have a blue poppy in your rock garden, try instead *M. quintuplinervia*, the harebell poppy from the mountains of China and Tibet. Only 45cm (18in) tall, its pendant cup-shaped lavender-blue flowers will look far more authentic in a rocky background and should prove longer-lived than its taller blue cousins, which tend to die after flowering in dry shallow soils.

In fact all these plants, even when naturally adapted to drought, would benefit from having a little organic matter worked into their crevices before planting, together with an occasional watering during summer drought.

from top to bottom *Asplenium ruta-muraria* (wall rue), *Meconopsis cambrica* (Welsh poppy) and *Meconopsis grandis* (Himalayan blue poppy).

plants for a rock garden

rock and scree plants

Campanula cochleariifolia
fairies' thimbles
height 8cm (3in).
spread 30cm (12in).
habit Hardy rhizomatous herbaceous perennial.
season Flowers June—August.
site Full sun or light shade, in moist gritty soil or scree.
characteristics Tussocky rosettes of small fresh green rounded leaves, spreading underground by slender runners. Hundreds of pendent bell- or thimble-shaped flowers appear all summer, sometimes into autumn, on delicate thread-like stems, in colours ranging from white, through various shades of blue to lavender.
how to grow Plant in spring in pockets of well-drained soil. Pull up unwanted runners to confine spread.
note Most rock garden campanulas are valuable for providing masses of colour after the main spring flush of bloom is over.

Cytisus x beanii
dwarf broom
height 15—40cm (6—16in).
spread 60—90cm (2—3ft).
habit Semi-prostrate hardy deciduous shrub.
season Flowers April—May.
site Full sun, in well-drained soil on ledges and in scree.
characteristics Small narrow hairy leaves clustered around arching or trailing stems, and lavish sprays of bright golden yellow pea-like flowers.
how to grow Sow in situ or plant from small pots in spring (older plants resent root disturbance). Prune very lightly after flowering, if necessary, and avoid cutting into old wood; plants flower on the previous year's stems.
note Even shorter is the slightly later flowering C. decumbens, a dense mat-forming species from the Apennines and Balkans.

Dianthus pavonius
(syn. D. neglectus)
alpine pink
height 5—8cm (2—3in).
spread 15—20cm (6—8in).
habit Hardy mat-forming evergreen perennial.
season Foliage all year; flowers June—July.
site Full sun, in well-drained acid soil and scree.
characteristics Dense mats and cushions of fine grassy, grey-green rigid leaves, topped by 10cm (4in) stems of solitary bearded blooms, up to 3cm (1¼in) across and varying in colour from pale pink to deep rose with a light buff reverse.
how to grow Sow or plant in early spring, in gritty neutral to acid soil in small pockets or crevices — do not bury the lower leaves. Deadhead after flowering to encourage dense growth.
note Many dianthus are worth trying as rock garden plants, especially the tiny D. alpinus, a lime-loving species.

Dicentra cucullaria
Dutchman's breeches
height 15cm (6in).
spread 25cm (10in).
habit Hardy herbaceous perennial.
season Foliage spring—summer; flowers April—May.
site Light or semi-shade, in gritty well-drained soil.
characteristics Deeply divided ferny blue-green foliage that dies down soon after plants flower, and soft creamy-white moth-like blooms, tipped with yellow, on slender arching stems. The scaly roots need moisture in spring but well-drained, almost dry soil in summer.
how to grow Sow or plant in early spring. Avoid disturbing roots when plants are dormant in summer.
note Early leaf growth can be frosted, so make sure plants are sheltered all round by rocks.

Leontopodium alpinum
edelweiss
height 15—20cm (6—8in).
spread 10—15cm (4—6in).
habit Hardy evergreen perennial.
season Foliage all year; flowers April—June.
site Full sun, in very well-drained gritty alkaline soil.
characteristics A basal cluster of lance-shaped woolly leaves, with a few more embellishing the stems that bear the clusters of small yellowish-white daisy flowers, surrounded by a star-shaped arrangement of white bracts.
how to grow Sow or plant in spring on short-turfed ledges or in pockets of very gritty soil between rocks and paving stones. Protect from winter rain with a cloche or sheet of glass.
note The hairy foliage is very sensitive to winter dampness, and in wet areas it is often better to grow the more weather-proof L. haplophylloides.

Veronica prostrata
(syn. V. rupestris)
prostrate speedwell
height 15—20cm (6—8in).
spread 40—45cm (16—18in).
habit Hardy herbaceous trailing perennial.
season Flowers June—August.
site Full sun, in gritty well-drained soil.
characteristics Oval toothed leaves on a dense bright green mat of branching, almost prostrate stems, and short upright spikes of pale or brilliant sky-blue flowers; pink, white and deeper blue cultivated varieties are available.
how to grow Plant in spring in pockets of poor well-drained gritty soil.
note One of the easiest and least demanding rock plants. Another is the rock speedwell, V. fruticans (syn. V. saxatilis), an 8cm (3in) native of Scottish mountains.

Cytisus x beanii (dwarf broom)

Dicentra cucullaria (Dutchman's breeches)

Veronica prostrata 'Mrs Holt' (prostate speedwell)

crack and crevice plants

Aquilegia alpina
alpine columbine
height 30—45cm
(12—18in).
spread 30cm (12in).
habit Hardy herbaceous
perennial.
season Flowers
May—June.
site Full sun or very light
shade, in rich well-drained
soil.
characteristics An
elegant plant with a mound
of finely divided feathery
blue-green foliage and
slender stems bearing
nodding blue or white
flowers with short spurs.
May be short-lived but
self-seeds readily (seeds
can take a year or more
to germinate).
how to grow Sow or
plant in spring, in crevices
packed with rich gritty
soil-based compost. If you
want to collect seeds,
keep away from other
species as they are prone
to cross-fertilization.
note In smaller rock
gardens, try *A. discolor*,
a native of Spanish screes
and just 10cm (4in) tall.

Erigeron aureus
fleabane
height 10cm (4in).
spread 15cm (6in).
habit Hardy herbaceous
perennial.
season Flowers
July—August.
site Full sun or light shade,
in well-drained soil pockets,
walls and pavements.
characteristics Tufted
mounds of hairy grey-
green spoon-shaped
leaves and short-stemmed
bright yellow daisies, up to
2.5cm (1in) across and
with rich golden centres,
opening from purple-black
hairy cup-shaped buds.
May be short-lived, but the
variety 'Canary Bird' is
more enduring.
how to grow Plant in
spring, with plenty of grit
to ensure sharp drainage.
Deadhead after flowering.
note Although not a true
rock garden plant, the
familiar Central American
species *E. karvinskianus*
(syn. *E. mucronatus*) is a
cheerful spreading and
self-seeding fleabane for
rocky edges and ledges.

Linum arboreum
evergreen flax
height 25—30cm
(10—12in).
spread 30cm (12in).
habit Hardy dwarf
evergreen shrub.
season Foliage all year;
flowers May—August.
site Full sun, in rich very
well-drained soil.
characteristics A loose
branching dwarf shrub,
with thick blue-green
bluntly elliptical leaves
and terminal bunches or
rosettes of bright lemon-
yellow funnel-shaped
blooms that open in
succession all summer.
how to grow Plant in
spring in pockets of gritty
soil with a little added leaf-
mould or other humus.
May be damaged by cold
wet winters, so take semi-
ripe summer cuttings.
note Several herbaceous
flax species are good rock
garden plants, including
evergreen rich yellow 15cm
(6in) high *L.* 'Gemmell's
Hybrid' and luminous blue
L. narbonense, 30—45cm
(12—18in).

Salix helvetica
Swiss willow
height 60cm (2ft).
spread 40—45cm
(16—18in).
habit Hardy dwarf
deciduous shrub.
season Foliage
spring—autumn; flowers
March.
site Full sun, in moist soil
in deep crevices or screes.
characteristics A dense
well-branched shrub with
upright stems. The grey-
green leaves are small and
oval, smooth above and
downy silvery-white
beneath. Heavy crops of
5cm (2in) long catkins
turning from silvery-white
to yellow as they mature.
how to grow Plant in
spring or autumn, in gritty
well-drained soil (not
chalk) with a little extra
humus.
note The various dwarf
willows have a range of
exciting catkin colours,
from golden yellow
(*S. apoda*) to burnt orange
(*S. retusa*) and even deep
purple-red (*S. alpina*).

Sorbus reducta
height 30cm (12in).
spread 30—45cm
(12—18in).
habit Hardy deciduous
suckering shrub.
season Foliage
September—October
(autumn tints); flowers
May; berries late summer
onwards.
site Full sun or light
shade, in well-drained
neutral or acid soil.
characteristics A sturdy
thicket of upright branches,
bearing finely divided
leaflets, normally dark
green but turning rich red
and purple in autumn. Flat
8cm (3in) heads of small
white flowers are followed
by conspicuous crimson
berries that age to pinkish
white. Plants sucker freely.
how to grow Plant in
spring or autumn. Pull up
or trim off suckers if these
are a nuisance.
note The only really
miniature mountain ash,
which remains dwarf in
crevices and poor soil;
in open rich ground, it
can reach 1.5m (5ft)!

Viola cornuta
horned violet
height Up to 30cm (12in).
spread 40—45cm
(16—18in).
habit Hardy evergreen
rhizomatous perennial.
season Flowers
May—August.
site Full sun or very light
shade, in pockets of rich
shade.
characteristics Dense
mats of long stems, at first
prostrate but turning up
at their ends, and small
fresh green pansy-like
leaves. Abundant short
stems of lively clear violet
or lavender-blue flowers
with simple white markings
and short spurs. Plants
may be short-lived but
self-seed freely.
how to grow Plant in
spring in a mixture of grit
and leaf-mould. Deadhead
regularly for longer
flowering. Propagate from
tip cuttings, or transplant
self-sown seedlings.
note The variety 'Minor'
or 'Alba Minor' are similar
but smaller, at only 8cm
(3in) high.

Aquilegia alpina (alpine columbine)

Erigeron aureus (fleabane)

Salix helvetica (Swiss willow)

a season

in the natural rock garden

Provided you have fitted together all the essential pieces of the rock garden jigsaw to create the environment these specialized plants require, you should find that keeping them happy involves less seasonal work than other kinds of natural gardens. A lot of rock plants have a reputation for being elusive, difficult or simply short-lived. True, the lives of some could be described as short and brutal, hardly surprising considering what they have to put up with, and perennial is a relative term that may mean a few years or longer than a human lifetime.

But remember that these species have had thousands of years of practise at surviving all that nature can throw at them, and in most cases injury or sudden death in the domestic rock garden is due to poor or inadequate preparation or positioning of the site in the first place. Get the drainage, exposure to light and shelter from excessively wet weather right, and you are almost certain of success. Seasonal care depends on maintaining these spartan conditions in alien lowland surroundings where elements unusual in the mountains – trees, mild winters and lack of snow protection, for example – might undermine the otherwise naturally robust constitution of rock garden plants.

spring

sowing – If you want a wide range of species in the garden, you will probably have to raise many of them yourself from seed or go to a specialist supplier, since garden centres rarely stock more than a basic selection of familiar kinds. These are popular because they are easy and reliable, and it is a good idea to start your collection with these, but as interest grows you might want to explore less common treasures such as soldanellas, the dainty snowbells of the high Alps, for example, or gentians, the typical mountain gems of limestone soils. Collecting ripe seeds from your own plants is also a sound insurance against their sudden demise.

You can start seeds in autumn, leaving them exposed to the subzero temperatures many need before they will germinate, or you might find it easier to sow very early in spring, when seedsmen and specialist societies are distributing their new seeds stocks, and the weather is likely to improve and favour rapid growth. Sow them thinly in pots or trays of soil-based seed compost mixed with an equal amount of fine grit, and stand the containers outdoors where they can experience one or two frosts. Make sure you cover them with wire mesh or netting to keep mice and birds at bay.

Then you can either leave them in the open until the seedlings emerge and need pricking out, or move the containers to a cold frame where they might be safer from disturbance. Don't be impatient – some appear very quickly, while others need a whole season or two before they will germinate. Once seedlings are large enough to handle, prick them out into trays or small pots of gritty soil-based compost, and grow on in the usual way. They will be ready for transplanting to their new homes in the autumn or following spring.

planting – I have something of a deserved reputation for packing as many plants as possible into the available space because I enjoy creating a rampant riot of growth and colour quickly. Rock garden planting is the antithesis of this, however; most of the species are individualists and each delicate mound of foliage and flower should be given room to display its glory in isolation. Even though I might plant several of the same genera together to make confident flowing drifts, I still leave enough space in between to be able to appreciate the special beauty of each one. This is the way alpines are found in their natural habitat and they are not natural competitors, so personal space is important.

The ideal time to plant, of course, is while you are building a rock garden. You can then position the plants on their sides at the edge of one stratum or layer of rocks before placing the next layer on top and packing the spaces all round with a gritty soil mixture. When planting in an established structure, you will need to excavate a hole large enough for each plant to sit comfortably at the same level as it was growing before – never bury them any deeper, because they are liable to rot off at the neck. Use small plants or seedlings for narrow cracks and crevices, pot-grown plants for larger cavities, ledges and scree beds where you can make the holes large enough. Firm the compost around each plant after setting it in place, and then spread a generous top-dressing of grit to aid drainage.

feeding and top-dressing – It stands to reason that small low-growing plants that do not naturally make rapid spurts of growth have little need for extra nutrients, and in the vast majority of cases there is no point in adding fertilizer at planting time, even on relatively barren soil. The only feeding rock plant

cuttings

▨ **To remove a dead rosette from the centre of a succulent plant, carefully insert a sharp knife and cut it cleanly through at its base, without disturbing the rest of the plant. Fill the gap left afterwards with some grit, to prevent weeds from colonizing the space while the plant grows back again.**

▨ **Many rock species such as gentians, violas and veronicas can be propagated by 'poor man's cuttings', produced when the donor plant spreads sideways, its shoots rooting as they go. Gently tease some of these rooted stems from around the edges, and repot them in gritty compost.**

▨ **When buying alpines, check carefully to make sure there are no signs of yellowing, which is often caused by over-watering or nutrient deficiencies. Make sure too that the roots are not forcing their way out of the bottom of the pot, a sure sign that the plant is pot-bound.**

▨ **Planting in a vertical crevice can be tricky. First wedge a stone in the crack, add some gritty compost and then gently feed the plant's roots in above the stone. Push another stone on top of the plant, pack more compost into any remaining space, and then water carefully to avoid washing away any of the soil.**

enthusiasts tend to do is give established plants a light sprinkling of bonemeal in early spring. This has the benefit of breaking down very slowly, delivering tiny amounts of nutrients throughout the growing season and avoiding the risks of stimulating unnaturally soft fresh growth that might be vulnerable to bad weather.

Immediately after giving this feed, you can top up any mulches of grit or other stony aggregates. These are bound to be disturbed during the season – birds toss the material around, planting and weeding bring soil to the surface, and heavy rain can scour some of the protective covering downhill. Weed around the plants and remove any self-sown seedlings for transplanting elsewhere, then spread fresh grit or gravel to bring the depth of mulch up to about 5cm (2in). As well as looking authentic and helping with drainage, you will find this is one of the best deterrents against slugs and snails, possibly the main pests of alpines.

Keeping rock gardens happy involves a lot less seasonal work than other kinds of natural gardens.

summer

watering – Ironically, most of the plants that depend on impeccable drainage for survival also require a regular supply of moisture during the growing season. Even high summer in the mountains and on cliff-tops has its damp days, and drought is often more common in winter, when the ground can be frozen for weeks on end but plants are fortunately dormant, than during the summer while plants are in active growth. It is important, therefore, to provide a regular supply of water should there be prolonged summer drought, applying enough to trickle down between the stones and top up the natural reservoir below. If possible, use collected rainwater rather than mains supplies for this purpose, because it will be free from lime, which the numerous ericaceous (acid-loving) alpine species detest.

weeding – Even though the conditions might seem thoroughly inhospitable, unfortunately weeds will appear sooner or later. Tiny opportunists like bittercress and spiderwort are common imports on bought plants, while many weed seeds drift for miles on summer breezes. They are best tackled while they are small – digging out a fanged dandelion root can disturb a large area of carpeting plants or carefully laid scree. Pull them up or gently tease them out by the root with a table fork, and then restore the mulch with an additional handful of fresh grit. Larger weeds, like dandelions and plantains, are best spot-treated with a systemic herbicide such as glyphosate, painted on their leaves as a gel which will avoid damaging nearby plants.

trimming and deadheading – You might not expect self-sufficient plants from high and inaccessible places to need the kind of tidying needed for more cosseted lowland species, and many of them look small enough without being trimmed any further, but in the wild they are often cut back regularly by grazing animals such as goats and hares, and by exposure to high winds, which often cause a form of pruning by killing buds and growing tips. This is one of the reasons why displays of mountain flowers can be so spectacular – hard pruning prompts a great flush of new growth, producing many more flowering shoots for the following year.

Simply trim off about one-third of the growth from mat and cushion-forming plants and branching shrubs with one-handed shears or even a pair of scissors. You can do the same to rampant or invasive species to limit their spread, but do not clip succulent plants and those with just a few rosettes unless they are too large. Deadheading faded blooms conserves energy needed for growth as well as tidying the plants, and can also stimulate another, smaller flush of flowers. Do not deadhead any required for seeds, nor those with decorative seedheads like Pasque flowers or mountain avens.

autumn

This is almost a repeat of spring, except that you need to keep one eye on the approach of winter. You can sow ripe, freshly collected seeds now and leave them outside until the spring, and also add new plants to the garden, either those you have raised during the season from spring sowings, or new ones you have bought in. It is also the time to dream and plan, whether you are contemplating extending or modifying the rock garden, or simply exploring seed catalogues before sending off your order.

pre-winter care – In November you should start thinking about protecting the more vulnerable species against winter rain and dampness. Assemble materials such as cloches, sheets of glass, dying fern fronds and fallen pine needles that you might need in a month or two, and watch out for accumulations of tree leaves. They can be lethal, so do not leave them lying for long over the tops of your plants, especially those with hairy leaves that tend to collect moisture. These include helichrysum and meconopsis species, edelweiss and many primulas. Gather up all the collected leaves and stack them in a wire mesh container or pack them in black plastic bags to rot down into leaf-mould, the best compost ingredient for those rock plants that need moist growing conditions.

winter

protection – This can be the most vulnerable period for all the rock garden plants. Out on the cliffs the frosts of winter are ameliorated by the ambient temperature of the sea, and in the mountains the plants are covered with a protective layer of snow. In the majority of British gardens, however, winter is a mild or damp season, exactly what these plants dislike. Few like sitting in cold damp soil as this causes crowns to rot off, and species that grow in the form of rosettes have leaves positioned to gather water and direct it back towards the crown. This is ideal when water is short, but can be a problem in a damp climate, especially if the foliage is also hairy.

The most effective help you can give the plants is to grow them in the first place in the right kind of free-draining soil, at an angle that will shed water and on a slope to encourage drainage away from their planting positions. As a further aid, shield hairy-leaved plants overhead with a sheet of glass or rigid clear plastic. Arrange a couple of bricks, one either side of the plant so that the sheet does not actually touch its foliage, or surround the plant with a ring of fern leaves or pine needles and rest the covering on that. Make sure it tilts slightly to one side, so that the rain can pour away and that it is held firmly in place with a few stones or lengths of wire attached to pegs driven into the ground as a precaution against high winds.

Far from being the alpines' enemy, a covering of snow acts as an insulator for the worst of the winter months.

the natural

The natural water garden is a complex and highly specialized environment and one that is more fragile than many other areas of the landscape. Recreating the natural diversity of a water garden can be challenging but also very effective.

water garden

origins

of the natural water garden

From its precipitation on the ground as rainfall to its destination at sea level, water is spurred on by the force of gravity in its permanent quest to find the lowest point in the landscape. Streams and rivers are constantly flowing downhill to estuaries, where the fresh water meets and mingles with the salty sea, the largest water body of them all. Smaller water features occur *en route* wherever that downward momentum is temporarily or permanently interrupted, resulting in a broad array of natural water gardens that can vary in Britain from the grand lakes of Cumbria, through white water rapids in the rivers of mid-Wales to the intermittent dew-ponds of Worcestershire. These are permanent features, which can be supplemented by seasonal water bodies that may only be obvious in winter or after heavy rainfall.

It is important at this stage to distinguish between a water garden and a wetland (see pages 74–99). This is sometimes obvious: a lake quite clearly has all the appearance of a water garden, whereas a marsh is undoubtedly a wetland. But these are extremes, and there are many types of wet zone that might be one or the other, depending on water depth, permanence and the kind of plants that grow there naturally.

For the purposes of this book I have chosen to distinguish between the two by treating as a water garden any area that *permanently* supports an open body of water. The level of the water may change, but the flora and fauna to be found there are totally reliant on its constant presence. Any area where water gathers in abundance, but only *occasionally* in sufficient quantities to create a body of open water, can be regarded as a wetland or damp garden.

For the natural water garden to thrive, a whole range of complex and often fragile components need to be present in the right quantities. Take the water itself, for example.

The vertical elegance of plants such as the flag iris can be perfectly reflected in still or slow-flowing water if they are planted at its margins.

In the vast majority of natural water gardens, it is continually moving from an entrance point to an exit in its ceaseless downhill course, and yet the garden depends for its existence on a permanent reservoir of a fairly constant depth. So more water must be supplied as fast as it drains away, while some kind of obstruction needs to be in place to restrict or dam its passage.

There are various kinds of natural barriers. In many cases these are relics of the last Ice Age ten thousand years ago, when glaciers swept down and between the sides of mountains, gouging out rock and carving large U-shaped valleys. Rocks and sediments were pushed along by the moving ice, which eventually retreated, leaving behind piles of debris at the ends or sides of the valleys. As water started flowing once more in the milder post-glacial climate, these rock piles created natural dams, behind which many of the lakes in Scotland, Cumbria and Wales were formed.

That is one way natural water gardens develop, especially those on higher ground or in valleys. Permanent bodies of water will also form where there is an underground layer of impermeable material. Many very hard metamorphic and igneous rocks, such as those found in the Scottish Highlands and Snowdonia, were the result of volcanic activity or massive heat and pressure from earth movements, which melted and compressed the rock particles until they were so dense that little or no water was able to percolate through. Wherever these rocks are present, drainage is impeded so that a high-water table develops, creating conditions in which ponds and lakes can form.

In the lowlands, on the other hand, even porous rocks can support water bodies. Sea-level is a natural boundary for flowing surface water, and wherever the ground is higher than this, a barrier is essential to stop its irresistible down-hill movement. At the lowest levels, however, rocks become saturated with water that has nowhere to drain to, resulting in a high water-table that surfaces wherever minor topographic undulations and valleys dip below sea-level.

These are the three commonest natural mechanisms by which the passage of water is interrupted, creating lakes or ponds and also suggesting ways by which a gardener can create a water garden. The mere presence of water is not enough on its own. It might offer movement and inspire breathtaking features such as falls, shoots and spouts, all of which have been mimicked and engineered into impressive garden features over the centuries, but these all lack one key element: life.

The life in any body of water is supported by oxygen, an essential element without which the flora and fauna struggle to survive and the water itself stagnates. Oxygen naturally finds its way into the water by two main routes. In the first place, it is extracted from the air by the water's own movement as it

cascades over rocks and falls. Writhing and foaming across the rough surfaces, it traps tiny air bubbles, almost invisible to the human eye but enough to supply the water with vitality. Certain aquatic plants also release oxygen from their leaves. These are oxygenators (see pages 58–63), not perhaps the most glamorous of species but essential as an alternative source in slow-moving or relatively still lakes and ponds where little oxygen is absorbed by physical turbulence.

Plants perform several other vital functions in addition to oxygenating the water. Their extensive networks of fine roots can bind the soil together, helping to maintain the structural stability of the beds and banks that define the watercourse. Floating species like the tiny lesser duckweed (*Lemna minor*) can cover the surface with a blanket of foliage that provides shade for many amphibious and aquatic creatures, and also helps moderate the temperature fluctuations caused by direct sunshine.

As on land, plants can only exist if their roots are able to extract nutrients from their surroundings. Some aquatic plants such as the free-floating frogbit draw food directly from the water, but the majority of water-garden plants follow the example of terrestrial species, absorbing nutrients contained within soil. Unlike in fast-flowing mountain streams, where the high water velocity scours and

carries away soil particles, the relatively modest speed of lowland lakes and watercourses allows deep soil deposits to build up and support some rather impressive plants, as we shall see.

Some of the most dramatic, such as the yellow pond lily (*Nuphar lutea*) with its breathtaking fragrant golden goblets, tend to be whole-hearted sun-lovers, spreading into lush rafts of foliage across the surface of brightly lit water. Sunlight is important for helping to maintain a healthy water eco-system, with essential oxygenators flourishing wherever light penetrates the depths of the pond. Despite their undeniable charm or drama, rocky gorges or deeply shaded woodland are not the places to look for water gardens full of colourful flowers, for these grow best in calm, open-water bodies where a proportion of the surface is well lit by the sun.

This brief look at the natural water garden shows a complex and highly specialized environment, and one that is more fragile than many other areas of the landscape. Re-creating it in all its wonderful diversity can be a challenge, and very often including water as a feature in the garden starts out as a grand idea but ends as a green soupy mess. The key to success lies in translating all the essential elements from the natural environment to a garden context.

Irrespective of scale, water captures light and brings it to the heart of the landscape.

identifying

the potential water garden

Water reflects all the changes and characteristics of the surrounding landscape. Star-bursts of sunlight on a bright spring morning, a slow explosion of lush foliage and flower, the excited chatter of a babbling stream – a water garden can provide it all, and once you have gardened with water you will find it hard to be without this mercurial element.

Modern gardeners are not alone in their passion. Water has been a centrepiece in most of the great garden designs in history, from the springs and cool

When combined with carefully selected plants, water brings an enchanting quality to the garden.

waters of biblical and earliest Egyptian times, through the classic landscape creations of Capability Brown to the futuristic designs of Bernard Tschumi's *Parc de la Villette*. The water garden has been a symbol of refreshment in torrid heat and drought, a sign of status and flaunted wealth in medieval society, and now, in a more democratic and environmentally aware age, an endangered habitat that you can re-create in your garden as a magical changing world with a secret life of its own.

What usually happens is that gardeners visit natural water landscapes and come home so inspired by the stunning scenery and floral beauty that they quite understandably decide to translate a piece of it to their own garden by simply adding water, on the assumption that this is the only key ingredient. But, as we have seen, we need to look at the wider context to really get the most from it and help it to blend naturally into the garden. Visual inspiration has to be combined with practical lessons from nature, especially with regard to the fundamental problem of encouraging water to stay put.

You might be fortunate enough to have a stream or spring flowing through the garden. If so, all you need do is take a lesson from the last ice age and literally gouge out a hole where you want a pond, using the excavated earth to create a dam or a bund (an embankment like those raised along rivers and coasts for flood defence). In principle this is relatively straightforward, but you should first monitor the consistency of the water flow and check its origin, since it might come from a polluted source. There are also tight regulations against interrupting natural watercourses, and you should consult the relevant authorities before playing at glaciers.

Sometimes a naturally high water-table can help you make a pond, in the same way as a lowland lake may be created. If your ground floods after prolonged rain without any obvious external source of ground water, or if it simply feels boggy underfoot, dig out a test hole about 60cm (2ft) deep to see if, and how quickly, it fills with water. This is most likely to happen in low-lying areas where water-retentive clay underlies the soil. All you have to do then is excavate a naturally shaped pond and wait for it to fill up.

Most of us must imprison water in the garden by other means that mimic the natural features of a hard impervious rock base. Perhaps the commonest and simplest method is to dig out the pond site and then line the excavation with a flexible sheet made from a synthetic material such as PVC or butyl rubber. These are easily laid to the desired shape and can be effective for up to 20 years, provided the material is not exposed to direct sunlight. Waterproof concrete is another popular and slightly more permanent option, although in my experience making this look natural is something of a challenge.

water, water...

Like most small boys (and, I suspect, girls), I was always fascinated by water, whether I was paddling in Cornish rock pools or fishing with home-made nets in streams behind our house, and even now I am irresistibly drawn to water in all its forms.

Anyone who already has a garden water feature will, I am sure, share this passion. Water gardens positively teem with life, and no other element in your design provides such opportunities for diversity of plants and wildlife.

If you already have a natural area of water, your most prized gardening tool will probably be a pair of waders and your regular gardening companion could be an amphibian with a croak. And if your experience of water features stops at tiny trickles of water or spouting cherubs, think beyond them and be bold – there are endless possibilities for including water in your garden.

cuttings

■ If you are digging out a pond to lay flexible liner, cut a shelf about 30cm (12in) deep all round for a perfect site for growing marginal and shallow water plants. Remember to use a spirit level while building the pond, because water always finds the flat plane and will reveal uneven edges.

■ If you have difficulty finding fleece or fabric underlay to cover the soil beneath the pond liner, a thick layer of sand or even glass-fibre insulating material will do the job just as effectively.

■ Before adding a pump or rock island to the pond, cover that part of the liner with several layers of underlay material to make sure nothing sharp can make contact with it and puncture a hole.

■ Fill a pond made with a liner slowly, allowing the weight of the water to push the material down into the excavated shape, and check it regularly so you can arrange the spare material in neat creases around the sides as it settles into place.

Often the oldest ideas are the best, and if you were to ask the great 18th- and 19th-century landscapers how to create a water garden, they would answer 'with clay'. The process is really quite straightforward, and involves spreading layers of damp clay into an excavated hole until the lining is about 15cm (6in) thick, or you can lay pre-formed mats of bentonite clay, which swells considerably in contact with water. The clay is then compacted or 'puddled' to make it impermeable. Landscapers like William Kent and Capability Brown achieved this by herding dozens of cattle backwards and forwards across the clay bed; perhaps a modern equivalent would be to organise a pond party for friends, all wearing waders.

Whichever way you choose to confine water, there is a danger that it will stagnate unless you can find a way of oxygenating it. In the natural landscape the constant movement of water continuously replenishes its oxygen supplies, but this does not happen in a domestic pond without your assistance. There are two possible solutions: you can install an electric pump and fountain that will disturb and aerate the water as effectively as a babbling stream, or you can introduce a generous stand of oxygenating plants (see pages 66–7).

Since most artificial water gardens have little or no through-flow of water from a natural source, there is no opportunity for soil deposits to build up. You could grow aquatic plants in baskets of pond compost, but this is a relatively tame solution that will contribute little to the kind of vibrant, evolving pond eco-system you are trying to create. It is much better to line the base of the pond with soil into which aquatic plants can root. A layer about 15cm (6in) deep will be sufficient, providing a more natural habitat for flora and fauna and also protecting synthetic liners from penetrating light, so extending their useful life.

Make sure you only use the most impoverished and preferably barren subsoil for this lining – the deeper layers dug out while excavating the pond would be ideal. The reason for this is that most kinds of garden topsoil are too fertile and contain huge quantities of nutrients that are soluble in water, where they would provide a feast for algae, upsetting the natural balance of micro-organisms and producing an explosion of green cloudiness in the pond (see Spring, page 69). A good mixture of microscopic creatures is essential for a rich, healthy wildlife pond, though, and you can ensure this by acquiring a bucket of sludge from a friendly gardener with a similar water garden to yours. This will bring with it a plethora of life, although transporting a bucketful of pond water home in the car without spilling it may be more of a challenge than creating the pond itself.

Finally, remember the kind of aspect favoured by the best natural water gardens. Since the vast majority thrive in high light levels with plenty of sunshine for at least six hours each day, you need to avoid the deep or lasting

shade cast by overhanging trees and tall buildings. The temperature of water can fluctuate dramatically when it is heated by the sun, however, and in shallow ponds this may be extreme enough to inhibit the growth of aquatic life. You can stabilize conditions by making sure the centre of the pond is at least 90cm (3ft) deep, and by creating areas of local shade with floating foliage, covering about 30% of the surface area.

Now you are ready to don your waders and discover some of the specialized plants that live in the natural water garden!

For a truly natural effect, allow your plants to invade the water garden.

plants
of the natural water garden

The rich diversity of specialized plant life within a water garden knits together to form a community or eco-system that is as fragile as it is beautiful. The subject of water plants is a complex one, because it deals with species that have evolved to survive in a changing environment. Unlike terrestrial habitats, where plants as varied as oak trees and chickweed find homes in situations that are fairly stable, water plants need to cope with variable conditions that can leave them totally submerged or high and dry just a few weeks later. In adapting to these conditions, most have come to play a specific role in the life of the pond.

The blanket term given to water plants is *macrophytes*, and this covers every species that naturally lives only in water, from the primitive and diminutive liver-worts and tiny duckweeds to water lilies, with their wide, floating leaf-pads and glamorous flowers. Each makes a particular contribution to the pond eco-system and, whereas most terrestrial gardens are composed of plants selected almost exclusively for their beauty, the water gardener has one eye on the appearance of a particular plant and the other on its function within the water community.

For convenience, aquatic plants are usually classified according to the position or depth of water they normally occupy. Although this can ignore the fact that many of these species adapt easily to other, slightly different habitats, I have followed the familiar system and broken them down into three distinct groups: free-floating, submerged and rooted marginal. If you want to create the truly diverse and well-balanced mixture that is essential for a healthy water garden, you need to choose some plants from each of these groups.

free-floating plants

As their name suggests, free-floating species spend their entire life-cycles in the water without setting their roots into soil. They tend to be fairly primitive plants, often composed of no more than a couple of leaves and a short dangling root

that absorbs nutrients in solution in the water. This simple mechanism means that some species – such as frogbit (*Hydrocharis morsus-ranae*), which has tufted rhizomes to increase the root area in contact with water – can respond quickly to high nutrient levels, soaking up the dissolved nutrients to support their rapid growth and so helping to prevent an excessive build-up. In turn, they are themselves a rich source of food for other water-borne creatures.

They are some of the first plants to find their way naturally into a new pond, arriving as fragments washed downstream from other wet zones by flowing water or, like duckweed's tiny 5mm (³⁄₁₆in) leaves, by hitching a lift on the feet of ducks and other water birds. Once in position they grow and multiply with such speed and profusion that they compete with algae in a feeding frenzy for the soluble nutrients, and in the majority of cases win hands down. As their delicate film of leaves spreads across the surface, they create a protective covering, which filters bright sunlight and casts much-needed shade that helps stabilize water temperatures. Although they are mere water weeds, you can see they take the first important step towards establishing a balanced eco-system, creating conditions that allow more highly developed plants and aquatic fauna to set up home in the pond.

Do not be fooled by their dainty looks and modest size, though. Some of these footloose miniatures are potentially rampant invaders, the Vikings of the plant world. Whereas the broad-leaved pondweed (*Potamogeton natans*) is not particularly invasive, despite its plain, no-nonsense appearance, the stunningly attractive fairy moss or water fern (*Azolla filiculoides*) is a notorious thug for all its beguiling looks, and colonizes any patch of water so successfully that it has been known to clog entire watercourses. Heavy rain can break the delicate ferny leaves into tiny fragments that are carried far and wide on the wind to regenerate spontaneously wherever they touch water. So beware – these plants might be small but they can have an enormous impact.

cuttings

■ When estimating the number of oxygenators you need to buy for your pond, allow about five plants (usually one bundle) for every square metre of the water surface.

■ Water lilies must have full sun for most of the day, otherwise they only produce foliage and few or none of their lovely blooms. Position them in the sunniest part of the pond, well away from fountains and running water, which they detest.

■ Introduce new plants gradually to their recommended level by placing them first on a block with their foliage at the surface, lowering them deeper as they grow. A sudden plunge to full depth can deny the leaves the light they need, and they may rot away.

from left to right *Hydrocharis morsus-ranae* (frogbit), *Potamogeton natans* (broad-leaved pondweed) and *Azolla filiculoides* (fairy moss).

57

from left to right *Hottonia palustris* (water violet), *Trapa natans* (water chestnut) and *Ranunculus fluitans* (river water-crowfoot).

Nonetheless, they are most definitely the unsung heroes of the water garden. Most look less than promising when purchased but they are full of potential as pioneers, and should be the first plants you buy for the new pond. One of my favourites is the water violet (*Hottonia palustris*) which, despite its name, is not so much a violet as a primula, with its simple five-petalled flowers, white or soft lilac-pink and yellow-eyed, and finely divided foliage. It drifts just under the water during spring and summer, quietly but efficiently oxygenating the water, and then erupts at the surface as its blooms appear. It is best suited to deeper water because, given half a chance, it will root into the soil in the shallows or near the bank.

Common or greater bladderwort (*Utricularia vulgaris*) is a peculiar plant that to my mind resembles a sea monster in behaviour. It lurks half-submerged, absorbing carbon dioxide from the water to keep itself afloat, and looks like a mass of green threads studded here and there with swollen flask-shaped bladders. It has few roots, and derives all its nourishment by catching small water creatures in these bladders, where they are decomposed by enzymes into plant foods such as nitrogen. Its flowers are remarkably attractive for such a sinister beast, and resemble small golden-yellow snapdragons as they protrude above the surface in the early summer sunlight. It is an excellent oxygenating plant, especially in warm, still, slightly acid water that is rich in the microscopic animal life on which it depends.

Water gardeners in mild climates might like to try the water chestnut (*Trapa natans*), often seen on the menu of Chinese restaurants. This is an annual, with handsome, almost geometrical rosettes of diamond-shaped foliage that float

freely, supported by the swollen leaf stalks. It has small white flowers in summer, raised above the surface on long stalks and followed in the autumn by hard black fruit, if you are lucky. These are starchy and have been used for food since the times of ancient lake-dwellers, but don't try eating them raw. If you do get fruits, store them indoors over winter in a bowl of cold water and replace them in the pond after the last spring frosts. There they will germinate and develop long stems that anchor them to the bottom while they are seedlings, decaying when the surface leaves start to develop.

submerged plants

These are the submariners of the water garden, spending their entire lives with their roots and crowns at the base of the pond, sometimes as much as 2m (6½ft) below the surface. Like *Trapa natans*, the seeds of plants such as the river water-crowfoot and arrowhead float to the bottom of the water and embed themselves in the soft silt and mud, but these plants remain rooted rather than breaking free to float at the surface, as the water chestnut does. Their roots and shoots are soft and fleshy, and many rely on their buoyancy in the water for structural support.

Some are able to survive in the reduced light levels well below the surface. The river water-crowfoot (*Ranunculus fluitans*), for example, has completely submerged foliage in bundles that stream out like locks of hair in fast-flowing rivers or down cascades where the water is rich in oxygen. Only its small white flowers appear at the surface in summer.

Arrowhead (*Sagittaria sagittifolia*), on the other hand, has three kinds of leaves. While it is growing, its foliage is thread-like and completely submerged, but later oval, floating leaves develop at the surface where they can absorb much needed sunlight. Just before its gorgeous white purple-eyed flowers open in late summer, the distinctive aerial arrow-shaped leaves that give its name rise up to 75cm (30in) above the water.

These submerged or bottom-rooting plants are multi-functional. Some, like the hornworts (*Ceratophyllum demersum*, and its rarer cousin *C. submersum*), are modest and spend their entire life lounging at depths where their underwater lawns of fine foliage oxygenate the water and breathe life into the pond. Others, such as spiked water milfoil (*Myriophyllum spicatum*), stabilize mud sediments with their roots, and most offer refuge, places to spawn and even food to pond fauna. All help produce the vital ingredient of shade that the water and its inhabitants need at the brightest times of the season. The common white water lily (*Nymphaea alba*), for example, buries its roots firmly in the mud, but produces long leaf stalks that reach up to the air, where its broad pads provide cool shade below and support on the surface for frogs, dragonflies and other resting creatures.

One unusual aquatic plant has a foot in both camps, since it is at the same time a free-floater and a bottom-rooter. The water soldier (*Stratiotes aloides*) is a hardy native perennial that always excites comment from gardeners new to water gardening when it suddenly vanishes from sight in winter. This Jekyll and Hyde plant spends the summer basking on the surface, producing delicate white three-petalled flowers and floating rosettes of serrated leaves, which

resemble heads of pineapple foliage and often expand into dense colonies. But, come the winter, they subtly adjust their buoyancy and descend into the murky depths where they form an oxygenating carpet on the bottom, safe from the threat of frost. It is a highly decorative plant, well worth adding to the water garden, especially since it is becoming rare in the wild.

Many submerged and bottom-rooting plants are particularly showy, and there is a large range for you to choose from when deciding what to grow in a pond. Water lilies are the classic water garden plant, with flowers of matchless beauty, but you need to take great care when deciding which of the countless varieties to introduce into the natural water garden.

Nymphaea 'Gonnère', for example, is one of the most magnificent lilies, with almost perfect, double white floating blooms, each one enhanced by vibrant yellow stamens. In a formal pond up to 1m (3⅓ ft) deep it can be a breathtaking centrepiece, but there is a danger that its enormous blooms may look contrived and out of place when mingled with other, more natural water garden species. Less flamboyant small-flowered nymphaea cultivars are just as decorative and blend more comfortably into their surroundings.

White *N.* 'Marliacea Alba' or canary yellow *N.* 'Marliacea Chromatella' are vigorous enough for natural ponds, but with simpler, less exotic flowers. For smaller ponds, compact species of *Nuphar*, the hardy pond lily, have fragrant yellow blooms and a more natural appearance – try *N. japonica* or, where the water is less than about 30cm (12in) deep, the really dwarf *N. pumila*. Instead of traditional water lilies, you might prefer to grow *Nymphoides peltata*, variously know as water fringe, floating heart or the fringed water lily (though it is a

from left to right *Nymphaea* 'Gonnère', *Stratiotes aloides* (water soldier), *Nymphaea alba* (white water lily) and *Nymphoides peltata* (fringed water lily).

relative of the bogbean and not a true lily). This is a native of still and slow-moving water bodies, with floating heart-shaped leaves and simple sun-shine-yellow blooms that are delicately fringed along the edge of every petal.

Another European perennial that looks totally at home in the natural water garden is branched bur-reed (*Sparganium erectum*) a common native of calm water, with grassy aerial or floating ribbon-like foliage that is usually evergreen. In summer it produces the most unusual branching flower spikes studded with several globe-shaped blooms on each stem, the smaller males at the top of the spike, above the larger females which, when fertilized, produce round prickly green fruits. Given time for the plants to establish themselves, these flower spikes can reach up to 1.5m (5ft) in height.

Far less imposing and seldom more than 60cm (2ft) high is water lobelia (*Lobelia dortmanna*), a bizarre relative of the familiar summer bedding plant, with submerged rosettes of foliage that do a wonderful job of oxygenating still, acid water. Only when in flower does it peep above the surface, sporting its slim leafless stems of tiny, pale, lilac, bell-shaped blooms from July to September. It is an easy-going perennial, growing happily in sunny pools with stony bottoms and a water depth anywhere between 10cm (4in) and 3m (10ft).

Finally, for an inspired touch of lavender blue in your scheme, you could not do better than to grow *Pontederia cordata*, with its less than glamorous common name of pickerelweed. It is anything but weedy, and in deeper sunlit parts of the pond produces rich green, spear- or heart-shaped leaves rising up to 75cm (30in) above the surface, with tiny pale blue or purple summer flowers

massed on tight conspicuous spikes. Grow this by itself, in bold groups so that you can enjoy it in all its glory, but make sure the water is at least 15cm (6in) deep because it is slightly frost tender. If grown as a marginal (see next group) its crowns should be covered with a mulch of leaves in autumn as an insurance.

rooted marginal plants

Rooted marginals are the species most of us picture when we think of aquatic plants. They crowd the banks and shallows of ponds and streams, producing an abundance of lavish architectural foliage and very often exquisite or eye-catching flowers, and blend seamlessly with plants of the wetland garden (see page 84). Some will spread towards the centre of the pond, especially if it is not too deep, or even survive out of water altogether, but they always produce a better show from the comfort of the pond margins. There they can paddle safely in shallow water less than about 30cm (12in) deep, and establish a network of firm fibrous roots that cling enthusiastically to the saturated soils at the pond edge, stabilizing them and countering the effects of erosion.

The vast majority have top growth that stands well clear of the water. Among the more statuesque of these is the common reedmace (*Typha latifolia*), which has long slender leaves – just 1–2cm (½–¾in) wide and characteristically sword-shaped – and dense cylindrical bulrush heads of brown female flowers, topped with a loose tuft of yellow male blooms. It can reach a height of 2–2.4m (6½–8ft), and spreads rapidly in still shallow water and on wet banks, often clogging a

from left to right *Sparganium erectum* (branched bur-reed), *Pontederia cordata*, (pickerel weed), *Typha latifolia* (variegated reedmace) and *Menyanthes trifoliata* (bog bean).

small pond in just a few seasons unless its invasive rhizomes are imprisoned in large planting baskets.

Some of its better-behaved cousins, such as the native lesser or narrow-leaved reedmace (*T. angustifolia*) or even smaller species like *T. laxmannii* and *T. minima*, barely 30cm (12in) tall, would be more restrained choices for smaller ponds. Another robust but less territorial plant that can cope with most marginal situations (see page 63) is bogbean or marsh trefoil (*Menyanthes trifoliata*) a charming lacy-flowered perennial found mainly in shallow water, but equally happy creeping up banks of wet acid soil.

Where the water or soil is more alkaline, you might find airy clumps of mare's tail (*Hippuris vulgaris*). Before you react with alarm at the prospect of introducing what you had always thought was a pernicious weed, I should explain that this is an appealing perennial that often suffers from mistaken identity. It bears shoots like miniature fir trees, about 30cm (12in) high on banks but much longer when submerged. A dainty plant that spreads at an easily controlled rate, it is quite unlike the visually similar horsetail (*Equisetum vulgare*), which can be a rampant thug if allowed space in the garden.

There are one or two select equisetums you can grow and still sleep peacefully at night. Like all horsetails they are ancient species, dating back to those distant times when coal measures were laid down, but they have learned self-control since then and will not spread into miniature forests, although you can confine them to planting baskets if you are still wary. The Dutch scouring rush, *E. hyemale*, grows 90cm–1.5m (3–5ft) high, with stiff, cylindrical, black-jointed stems and no recognizable leaves. There are no flowers either, because it is more like a fern, producing spores in 'cones' that appear near the tops of the stems. *E. variegatum* is similar, but only 75cm (30in) tall and with black, green and sometimes orange tips. Both plants flourish immersed in water up to about 15cm (6in) deep.

Water mint (*Mentha aquatica*) can enjoy twice this depth and will also spread enthusiastically into any wet soil, although you can control it by pulling off the horizontal stems rooting into the suface. Bees love its tight whorls of fragrant mauve flowers, and you can use its leaves as a substitute for peppermint. There is a curly-leaved form (*M. aquatica* var. *crispa*) while the normal wild species sometimes produces unusual, rich reddish-purple leaves on plants in full sun.

For a really colourful display at the pond margins, in water up to 10cm (4in) deep, it is hard to beat the North American cardinal flower (*Lobelia cardinalis*) with leaves somewhere between bronze and reddish-green and 90cm (3ft) tall spires of classy deep red flowers all summer. The best hybrid of this is 'Queen Victoria', whose fantastic blood-red foliage gleams in bright sunlight and turns almost regal purple at sunset.

If you think this is a little extrovert for the natural water garden, blend it in with a surrounding lawn of needle spike rush or hairgrass (*Eleocharis acicularis*), a slender plant with an architectural appearance and a dual personality. On muddy land it produces spreading tussocks of fine greenish brown foliage with delicate fluffy white flower-heads about 30cm (12in) tall. Under water, however, it is an efficient and unobtrusive oxygenator.

No wet site would be complete without an iris. Many prefer bog gardens and wetlands, where their rhizomes are clear of water, but some tolerate or even relish submersion, at least in summer, and top of this aquatic selection must be the Japanese flag iris, *Iris ensata* (formerly *I. kaempferi*). The simple wild species, a 90cm (3ft) tall plant with fleshy sword-like foliage and beardless flowers of reddish purple with a yellow blotch on each fall, has been coaxed, selected and manipulated into producing dozens of varieties in different colours and combinations, all making a breathtaking display in June and July. White 'Alba', greenish white 'Moonlight Waves', and the variously spotted and flecked Higo hybrids are elite choices for any water garden.

from left to right *Hippuris vulgaris* (mare's tail) *Equisetum hyemale* (Dutch scouring rush), *Mentha aquatica* (water mint) and *Iris ensata* (Japanese flag iris).

plants for a water garden

free-floating plants

Lemna spp.
duckweed

height Flat on water surface.

spread Indefinite.

habit Hardy floating or submerged perennial.

season Foliage spring–autumn.

site Full sun to moderate shade, on still water of any depth.

characteristics Tiny flat deciduous leaves, each with a single root, dividing frequently to form a floating colony. Flowers are minute and rarely produced in temperate climates. Plants often overwinter as submerged dormant buds.

how to grow Add plants to the water in spring, although they often cling to other aquatic plants or visiting birds. Thin plants if they become too extensive.

note Ivy-leaved duckweed (L. trisulca) is the prettiest species, while all others are more invasive, each tiny plant covering up to 1sq m (10sq ft) per year. An essential duck food!

Wolffia arrhiza
rootless duckweed, water meal

height Flat on water surface.

spread Indefinite.

habit Hardy floating or submerged perennial.

season Foliage spring–autumn.

site Full sun to moderate shade, on still water of any depth.

characteristics Minute thick round or oval green single leaf, barely 1mm (¹⁄₂₅in) across, without any root, and a microscopic flower in the centre of each leaf (never flowers in European ponds).

how to grow Treat in the same way as its close relative duckweed (Lemna), though colonies are seldom dense enough to need thinning.

note Thought by many botanists to be the smallest flowering plant yet identified – it is locally common in the wild, but often overlooked.

submerged plants

Callitriche palustris
(syn. C. verna)
water starwort

height Flat on water surface.

spread Indefinite.

habit Hardy floating or submerged evergreen perennial.

season Foliage all year.

site Full sun or slight shade, in still or slow-moving water 10–50cm (4–20in) deep.

characteristics Tiny oval evergreen leaves form star-shaped rosettes or narrow, spear-shaped oxygenating foliage. Plants attached to the mud by thread-like stems and fine roots.

how to grow In spring, bundle several stems together with a weight, and throw into the water. Needs little attention, but you can thin it every 2–3 years.

note This is the most commonly-sold species. Most widespread in the wild are common water starwort (C. stagnalis), and autumn starwort (C. hermaphroditica, syn. C. autumnalis).

Crassula helmsii
(syn. Tillaea recurva)
New Zealand pygmyweed

height Flat on water surface.

spread Indefinite.

habit Fairly hardy submerged, floating or occasionally marginal evergreen perennial.

season Foliage all year (summer in cold shallow water); flowers June–September.

site Full sun, in still water 25–90cm (10in–3ft) deep.

characteristics Evergreen needle-like foliage packed in rosettes on long branching stems that often float at the surface, and insignificant unstalked white or pink four-petalled flowers in summer. Plants creep and root along the pond bottom. A good oxygenator.

how to grow Drop weighted bundles of cuttings in the pond in spring. Thin every 2–3 years if invasive.

note Can become invasive in the wild, so make sure it stays in the pond.

Hydrocharis morsus-ranae
frogbit

height Flat on water surface; flowers 5–8cm (2–3in).

spread Indefinite.

habit Hardy floating or submerged perennial.

season Foliage spring–autumn; flowers June–August.

site Preferably full sun but tolerates light shade, in shallow, still, fairly alkaline water.

characteristics Floating 60cm (2ft) diameter rosettes of kidney-shaped leaves and white, yellow-eyed three-petalled flowers that rise on single stems above the water surface. Passes the winter as dormant bulbous buds on the pond bottom.

how to grow Drop young plants into the water in spring. Thin excessive growth occasionally.

note The terminal buds can be collected in a jar of water in September and overwintered in a frost-free place.

Nymphaea 'Pygmaea Helvola'

height Flat on water surface.

spread 30cm (12in).

habit Hardy rhizomatous submerged perennial with floating foliage.

season Foliage spring–autumn; flowers June–September.

site Full sun, in still water 10–30cm (4–12in) deep.

characteristics Floating lily pads about 6cm (2½in) across, deep olive-green with red or brown blotches, and 5cm (2in) canary yellow single blooms with golden orange stamens.

how to grow Plant the rhizomes in spring, directly in the pond mud or in baskets. Bury them at 45 degrees with their tips at the surface. Remove old leaves and flowers before they can rot, and divide plants every 3–5 years if they become overcrowded.

note A garden hybrid between the tiny N. tetragona and the Mexican yellow water lily, this is ideal for very small ponds.

Lemna minor (common duckweed)

Callitriche palustris (water starwort)

Hydrocharis morsus-ranae (frogbit) and *Nymphaea* 'Pygmaea Helvola'

Persicaria amphibia
(syn. *Polygonum amphibium*)
water bistort
height Flat on water surface (up to 75cm (30in) on land).
spread 60cm (2ft) in water; indefinite on land.
habit Hardy submerged, marginal or wetland perennial.
season Foliage spring–autumn; flowers July–September.
site Full sun or light shade, in water 30–45cm (12–18in) deep and in any wet soil.
characteristics Long spear-shaped deciduous aquatic leaves, floating in deep water or aerial in the shallows, neat dense spikes of deep pink flowers. Fairly docile in deep water, but rampant in shallow water and on land.
how to grow Plant in spring, directly in soil or in baskets. Pull up spreading roots to confine growth to deeper water.
note Self-seeds freely, so deadhead to limit spread.

Ranunculus aquatilis
common water-crowfoot, water buttercup
height Flat on water surface.
spread 1.5m (5ft).
habit Hardy floating or submerged perennial (occasionally annual).
season Foliage spring–autumn; flowers April–August.
site Full sun or semi-shade, in still or flowing water 5cm–1m (2in–3¼ft) deep.
characteristics Dark green floating leaves, rounded and deeply divided, and fine submerged leaves like grassy strands. Small white buttercup-like blooms with yellow centres held just above the surface on short stalks.
how to grow Plant in spring, directly in the bottom or in baskets. Thin by pulling or raking out stems if plants threaten to overcrowd others.
note Very vigorous, and popular with all pond creatures for food, shelter and spawning.

Butomus umbellatus
flowering rush
height Up to 1.5m (5ft).
spread 60cm (2ft).
habit Hardy rhizomatous marginal perennial.
season Foliage spring–autumn; flowers July–September.
site Full sun or light shade, in very wet soil or in still or slow-moving water up to 15cm (6in) deep.
characteristics Long narrow purplish-green leaves, triangular at their base and growing in bunches from thin spreading rhizomes. Spreading airy heads of soft pink flowers with red stamens, followed by rounded fruits that float to new sites.
how to grow Plant in spring, directly in the marginal mud or in planting baskets for smaller pools. Divide every 3–4 years.
note The protein-rich rhizomes are cooked or turned into bread flour in parts of Asia.

Calla palustris
bog arum
height 30–45cm (12–18in).
spread 30cm (12in).
habit Hardy rhizomatous marginal or wetland perennial.
season Foliage spring–autumn or evergreen; flowers June–August; fruits autumn.
site Full sun or light shade, in very wet soil or still water 15cm (6in) deep.
characteristics Thick heart-shaped leaves, each on a long stalk rising straight from the ground, and a spike of greenish yellow flowers surrounded by a white papery arum-like spathe, followed by a clustered head of bright red berries. Spreads slowly as thick creeping rhizomes.
how to grow Plant in spring in wet soil or in baskets. Can also be grown from the ripe berries, sown into the soil in autumn.
note The fruits are poisonous and can be very dangerous if eaten.

Myosotis scorpioides
(syn. *M. palustris*)
water forget-me-not
height 40cm (16in).
spread 60cm (2ft).
habit Hardy rhizomatous marginal or wetland perennial.
season Foliage spring–autumn; flowers May–September.
site Sun or shade, in moist soil, or still water 15cm (6in) deep.
characteristics Small hairy bright green leaves on branching stems (can be very long in aquatic sites), ending in clusters of tiny single bright blue flowers with conspicuous white or yellow centres. Spreads rapidly, but not invasively, by slender surface rhizomes.
how to grow Plant in spring or autumn in wet soil. Thin occasionally, or lift and divide every 2–3 years.
note Coleridge described it as the 'blue and bright-eyed flowerlet of the brook', although it was known as scorpion grass.

Saururus cernuus
lizard's tail, swamp lily, water dragon
height 1.2m (4ft).
spread 1.5m (5ft).
habit Hardy rhizomatous marginal or wetland perennial.
season Foliage spring–autumn, with late autumn tints; flowers June–August.
site Sun or shade, in damp soil, or in still or gently flowing water to 40cm (16in) deep.
characteristics Dense clumps of abundant large heart-shaped leaves, fresh olive green with a luminous underside and turning rich crimson in autumn, topped by drooping spikes of tiny creamy-white flowers, which are fluffy and fragrant. Grows and spreads slowly from creeping rhizomes.
how to grow Plant in spring, directly in the soil. If growing above water level, mulch every spring with garden compost.
note Its Latin name means 'curved lizard'.

Butomus umbellatus (flowering rush)

Myosotis scorpioides (water forget-me-not)

Saururus cernuus (swamp lily)

a season

in the natural water garden

Planting up a terrestrial border is normally quite a simple process because the majority of plants have a root system at one end and green top growth at the other. You can usually tell which is which, and planting them the right way up is rarely a problem: simply dig a hole, insert the rooted end, cover it up with soil, and the job is done.

Water plants are not so straightforward, though. Some appear to be nothing but root, and others have no root at all, while a few species, in their dormant state, look rather like a pile of slimy newspaper. Most are born survivors, able to adapt to any wet environment, and if you simply leave them at the water's edge many will drift, creep or seed themselves into their favourite positions. To give them a head start, however, it is useful to know the best way to plant them exactly where they prefer to grow.

Free-floating species such as bladderwort or water chestnut, and many submerged plants like hornwort or water fringe are easy to introduce to the pond. Launch them on the surface or toss them further out onto the water, and they will float off to find their own site where they can start multiplying and spreading into established colonies.

Submerged oxygenators like pondweed, milfoil and willow moss (*Fontinalis antipyretica*) are often bought as groups of cuttings, bundled together with a bent strip of lead. This weights them down, so they will sink into the bottom mud when you throw them into the water. You can often multiply your own plants in this way, simply gathering a handful of stems and tying them together with string attached to a small stone.

Other water plants, especially rhizomatous bottom-rooting or marginal species like water lilies or bog arum, need planting conventionally in soil. There are two ways to add them to the water garden. Perhaps the simplest is to plant them directly into the silt that has settled at the bottom of the pond, although this method can lead to problems eventually. Many water plants spread vigorously, some of them very invasively, and you might find you have released a horticultural vandal a season or two after allowing it free run of your pond. If this happens, be prepared to spend wet hours clearing vast amounts of over-enthusiastic foliage from affected parts of your water garden.

An alternative (and more controllable) method is to plant them in special plastic aquatic pots, which have a series of holes all round the rim to allow free passage of water through the rootball, while at the same time stopping the plant from spreading freely all over the pond. These pots also make it easy to lift an overgrown or geriatric plant out of the pond, allowing you to divide it and re-pot the young fragments in the same way as a terrestrial plant. Sit the pots on the bottom of the pond or, for plants that need shallower water, stand them on a marginal shelf or on a stack of bricks to raise them to their preferred depth.

It is important not to use ordinary potting compost mixtures when potting water plants, because these are formulated to meet the specific needs of ter-restrial plants and contain large amounts of nutrients, far too much for water plants and their surroundings. Most of the fertilizer would leach out into the water, encouraging the growth of algae and so fouling the pond. Instead use specially blended aquatic compost or weak soil from a barren part of your garden. It is also a good idea to top off pots with a layer of grit, which holds the soil in place as you lower the plant into the pond and discourages fish from nosing around a new plant, producing silty clouds in the water.

It is not usually necessary to feed water garden plants, unlike those growing in a conventional border. Your aim should be to create a self-sufficient eco-system where the flora and fauna provide each other with adequate nutrients, oxygen and shelter, and a sudden influx of nutrients could create an imbalance that might affect the whole community. Nutrients normally find their own way into the pond in the water that runs off the surrounding soil – sometimes to excess, as spring flushes of green water often demonstrate – and for this reason I tend never to apply rich fertilizers to plants around ponds.

spring

tidying – If the balance of plants in your water garden is right, just one serious maintenance session a year will be necessary. This will inevitably mean getting wet, so choose a pleasant day for the task!

Start by removing dead foliage, especially any floating on the surface. Spring is better than autumn for this, because the old top growth will have supplied a safety blanket of foliage over the crowns of dormant plants during winter. Now its usefulness is passed and you can clear it all away, although there is no need

From the first glimpse of sun in spring, the water garden abounds with life.

cuttings

▪ **Water lilies are particularly susceptible to aphids. Try washing them off with a jet from the hosepipe, and if that doesn't work lay wet sacking over the whole plant to submerge it for 24 hours.**

▪ **If you want to introduce fish or other aquatic creatures, float the bag they came in for a few hours on the surface to allow the water temperature inside to match that of the pond.**

▪ **When dividing water plants growing in plastic aquatic pots, don't try to pull the plant out because its roots will have pushed through the holes all round the sides. Instead cut the pot away in stages, gently teasing the roots from the holes to avoid injury.**

▪ **Be aware of chemicals you may be applying to other parts of the garden. Anything that remains active after coming into contact with the soil could be washed into the pond, with harmful effects, so always try to use an organic product.**

to scrabble around for every expired bit of leaf – the water garden is intended to be a natural environment where dead matter is part of the equation, so you are not trying to produce a clean and neat appearance. You can also haul out some of the pond weed if this seems to be occupying too much space – don't throw it away as it is a wonderful supplement for adding to the compost heap, but leave it lying at the waterside for a few days first so that any creatures buried within can find their way back to the pond.

If the pond seems overgrown, now is the time to decide what you are going to do about it. As explained elsewhere (see pages 76–7), soil deposits and accumulations of plant growth at the water's edge are all part of the natural pond dynamics, and in the long term will transform a water garden into a wetland with its own specialized flora and fauna. You will probably not want this to happen, and that is one of the reasons for this spring tidying session, but wholesale clearance can disrupt established communities of species, so it is best to tackle a really overgrown pond in stages. Just clear a few areas, or remove only a proportion of the plant growth – up to about one-third – so other parts are left untouched as sanctuaries for wildlife.

pests and diseases – While you are working among the plants, give them the once-over to check for signs of trouble, and remove any plants or foliage that have been affected. Most pests only start to build up in any numbers from late May or June onwards, however, and are rarely troublesome. The few that can be serious – such as water lily beetles, some water midges and aphids, which can transmit viral diseases – can be forcefully hosed off into the water, where many will be eaten by aquatic predators. Remember that in a natural garden, insects that might be pests elsewhere are often part of a complex food net or chain, with other creatures dependant on them for survival. It is anyway inadvisable to use chemical sprays near water, because their residues can affect other species.

green water – In newly established water gardens a curious phenomenon often occurs as spring arrives. Primitive single-cell algae begin to increase at a rapid rate, filling your pond with a concentrated green cloudiness or 'bloom' that may be so thick it stops light penetrating the water, which temporarily impedes the growth of all the other water plants. The algae are able to multiply so fast because the water is filled in spring with a great seasonal concentration of nutrients. While most plants were dormant over the winter, these food materials were surplus to needs and have gradually built up from water draining off the land. Algae are the first to respond when the water begins to warm up in spring, and they fatten on this soup of nutrients. Fortunately the phenomenon is short lived; the surplus is soon used up as other pond plants burst into life, and the algae die as quickly as they arrived.

summer

blanketweed – As well as causing this green bloom, the extra dissolved minerals can feed an explosion of other algae, this time the long filamentous species variously known as flannelweed, silkweed or blanketweed. These produce long hair-like strands that tangle together near the surface in huge mats. They do not always disappear as quickly as the single-cell algae and you may want to remove this covering if a large area of the surface is shaded. Plunge a garden rake or a long rough stick into the middle of the weed and wind it up into a great mass. It will be heavy while wet, so just drag it on to the bank and leave for a few days to drain before taking it to the compost heap.

weeding – Marginal areas just out of the water are fertile seed-beds for unwanted weeds and seedling pond plants. These wet zones can be unpleasant to weed in winter and virtually inaccessible later in the year, so check round during early summer to see if you need to clean up or thin some areas with a small handfork. Watch out for useful seedlings that can be transplanted elsewhere before the hot dry weather arrives, and make a note of any ageing perennials that need dividing and replanting next autumn or spring. This is also a good time to 'prune' invasive species by chopping off their meandering runners and rhizomes with a spade.

topping up – Water levels fluctuate naturally in almost every water garden, and most plants can cope with brief seasonal flooding or dry exposure, so there will rarely be any need as summer progresses to top up water levels in the same way for formal pools. If you have recently finished making a pond, you might have a natural spring or stream to fill it, or you could wait for rainwater to do the job. On the other hand, a combination of impatience and evaporation might tempt you at some point to reach for the hosepipe instead. In theory there is nothing wrong with this, but tap water is usually much colder than the water in your pond, possibly giving established aquatic life a lethal shock, and it is relatively high in nitrates, which can encourage the growth of algae. So my advice is to rely on collecting rainwater to top up your pond, and if you must use a hosepipe, leave it trickling very slowly indeed to allow the water time to warm up.

autumn

propagation – Towards the end of the growing season, while the ground and water are still warm, you can divide and replant many overgrown perennials, which will often settle in quickly and establish before winter arrives. If any of this work is uncompleted before the first frosts, it can be done as successfully in spring.

Dig up plants growing in the soil or pull up those rooted in the pond bottom, and tear, tease or cut them into smaller fragments. Discard old large woody pieces and keep only the younger outer portions for replanting as these are more vigorous. Plants growing in baskets can be lifted out of the water for dividing in the same way and repotting in fresh aquatic compost.

protection – Most ordinary garden ponds are covered with a net in autumn to keep falling leaves out of the water, which they can easily foul if they accumulate on the bottom. This is not so critical for natural ponds, where the decomposing leaves and leaf litter from the plants in and around the water will add nutrients and contribute to the bottom deposits in which your plants are rooting.

Some of these plants may need a little protection to help them get through the winter if they are slightly tender or you live in a cold district. Gunnera, for example, is frost-sensitive and will benefit from a thick covering of conifer branches, bracken or a mound of its own dying leaves. Insulate arum lilies (*Zantedeschia*) in the same way, or enclose them with a circle of wire netting filled with straw.

The first frosts will kill tender floating plants like water lettuce and water hyacinth (*Eichhornia crassipes*), so pull off some young portions and keep them indoors over the winter in a tank of mud and shallow water. Water lilies are hardy plants that normally survive winter unscathed where they are rooted in the bottom under water deeper than about 45cm (18in). Lilies in baskets in shallower depths could suffer, and it would be wise to lift their baskets, tidy any remaining foliage and then plunge them in containers of water kept in a frost-free greenhouse.

winter

hibernation – The natural water garden can usually look after itself during winter. Most plants will be dormant, and pond creatures are either hibernating or lurking in a semi-torpid state at the bottom of deeper ponds, where the temperature rarely falls below 4°C (39°F). Frogs, toads and newts pass the winter months out of the water, under stones and insulating layers of dead top growth – this is one of the reasons for not tidying up too thoroughly in autumn! You can help them survive by arranging small piles of stones near the pond or laying a stone slab over a scooped out depression in the ground.

frozen ponds – Freezing is seldom a problem unless the cold snap continues for weeks rather than days. Where ice is thicker than about 5cm (2in) and covers a shallow pond for any length of time, it is a good idea to free part of the surface to allow noxious gases from decomposing sediments to disperse.

Don't simply break the ice with a hammer, though, as this causes shock waves throughout the water and may concuss fish and other fauna. Instead, try levering up panels of ice near the edge with a metal bar, stand a tin on the ice and fill it with hot water, or keep a rubber ring floating on the surface and pour hot water inside this.

Finally, remember to visit the pond often in winter, if only to appreciate the frozen beauty of frost and ice on the plant growth that is still standing at the water's edge. On mild days you could find a surprising amount of activity going on, and before you know it, early buds breaking and the first flurries of frog and toad courtship will herald the arrival of another spring.

Even in the depths of winter the water garden possesses an ethereal quality.

the natural

Wetlands make for some of the most inspiring landscapes, embodying dramatic changes that have taken centuries to occur. The varied character of wetlands means that there is plenty of scope for re-creating wetland conditions in your own garden.

wetland garden

origins

of the natural wetland garden

For me this is one of the most dynamic and exciting types of landscape, where several vital growth needs are often fully satisfied. A plentiful supply of year-round moisture, good fertility and high light levels tend to occur most frequently in that narrow band where the fertile, well-drained soils of pasture and meadow meet the shores of lakes, streams and ponds. This damp territory is where you will find the natural wetland garden, a lush and verdant boundary between water and dry land, packed with plants that seem to exude a boundless zest for life.

This is a zone of transition, a perfect example of the way in which the landscape is constantly shifting. Technically it demonstrates succession from one environmental condition to another, a process that is taking place everywhere as landscapes evolve. In this instance it is the gradual change from open water to dry land – a soggy area of soil in your garden that will make a great wetland probably started life as a pond, stream or even a river.

On the face of it, this kind of change sounds dramatic, but it takes place very slowly and may have occurred centuries ago – or, of course, it may be happening in your garden even as you read this text. The principles are the same wherever there is flowing water, which is restlessly active and inevitably alters the immediate landscape.

A young, fast-flowing water course has the momentum to scour its bed and banks, moving the resulting rock particles and debris downstream, but as it ages it slows down, losing its ability to carry these particles, which sink to the bottom and build up as soil deposits. This is a continuous process, the deposits gradually accumulating as more particles are brought in and left by water flowing from the surrounding land.

As the soil depth in the watercourse increases, so plants that can cope with wet conditions begin to establish themselves, at first just here and there. The more successful pioneer plants flourish, multiply and spread, their roots and shoots restricting the water's passage and slowing its flow further so that even

more particles sink to the bottom, accelerating the build-up of deposits. As plants die, their leaves and stems decompose in the water, adding organic matter to enrich the new soil and allowing greater numbers of plants to flourish.

This process of soil deposition and accumulation occurs more rapidly in the relatively still water of lakes and ponds, in the absence of a natural fast flow that would otherwise carry the soil elsewhere. Ultimately all natural watercourses would silt up and become land if they were not scoured by a fast-moving current or artificially maintained by occasional dredging and bank maintenance to keep the water flowing. Ironically as one watercourse becomes clogged, the overflowing water scours an alternative route of less resistance, creating another stream, river or area of wetland where the same pattern of deposition and silting up will take place.

In fertile, moist conditions, plants bound with life, and with a carefully considered planting scheme a wetland garden can provide year-round colour and interest.

above and above right Even in extreme conditions, such as marl pits and clay salt marshes, water plants still thrive.

The soil that results from this creative process is usually perfect for garden plants. It varies tremendously in character from region to region, its precise composition being determined by the rock and soil through which the original watercourse flowed. The good news for gardeners is that it tends to be a well-structured soil, rich in organic matter from the decomposition of the plants responsible for congesting the watercourse, and high in nutrients, which were introduced in solution by the flowing water. It is a naturally healthy, firm soil that allows plant roots to penetrate easily in their search for anchorage and readily available food materials.

It will also vary widely in acidity or alkalinity, depending on the quality of the water flowing into the garden, where it comes from, and the type of plants already growing in your wetland area. A water-logged patch with masses of decayed plant materials, especially mosses, can produce a natural bog that may be very acid if nutrient levels are low. Where reeds and sedges replace mosses, it may be classed as a fen, with alkaline soil and a quite different selection of wetland plants. On the other hand, if there are very few plant deposits, it could be a marsh with comparatively good drainage because of the

lack of peat, and a soil that is either acid or alkaline. So it is important to carry out a soil test to check the pH and help you choose appropriate plants for your soil (see page 10).

In the natural landscape, the wetland garden can range in size from several hectares of valley floor to a slender strip perhaps only a few metres wide along the side of a stream or river. Its character can vary tremendously too, from permanently wet soil immediately beside the watercourse to more marshy land that is saturated infrequently, perhaps only during a winter flood, so there is plenty of scope for re-creating wetland conditions in your garden. Damp areas can be enhanced, extended or manipulated to provide the conditions moisture-loving plants enjoy. Most areas respond very well to comparatively little intervention on your part.

Many plant species native to natural wetlands can often tolerate fluctuations in conditions and a wide range of damp environments, but some are quite particular about their requirements, so my advice is to learn how to identify the key features of your site and how they can be adapted before departing for your plant supplier.

identifying

the potential wetland garden

Water is, of course, the key to this kind of landscape, and it might seem logical to expect all the best damp gardens to be confined to areas of high rainfall. Although this is often true, several other factors are also relevant to the success of the wetland garden.

More important than the quantity of rain is the amount of water that collects and remains in the soil. Water naturally flows downhill (but see page 48!), and so the bottom of slopes and valleys along the side of rivers and streams are often where nature's finest wetland gardens are to be found, and this can be some distance from where the rain first fell.

You may not garden close to a stream or river, but that does not mean the ground cannot be naturally damp. I have found great wetland gardens in the most unlikely of places, from urban jungles to the sides of wild and windswept mountains, and there is hardly anywhere in the landscape that can be automatically discounted.

Damp conditions can occur on the side of a hill, perhaps where a spring allows water to come to the surface from a natural reservoir trapped deep in the rock below. On the other hand, a glance at the local topography might reveal that your garden sits in a hollow or low-lying area where water could gather. These slight undulations in the landscape need not be cavernous, and often a dip of a few centimetres within a level garden is sufficient to create a bowl to collect water.

Whatever your geographical location, you might simply have the type of soil that naturally holds moisture long after other kinds have dried out. Water is only of use to plants if it is stored up in the soil, so the speed at which it percolates through is critical when determining whether you have, or can have, a damp garden. As we have seen, sandy soils are composed of large particles that allow water to escape quickly, whereas the small particles of heavy clays drain very gradually, making it available to plants for longer – too long in the case of species sensitive to water-logging, but perfect for wetland plants. If your soil also has plenty of organic matter from rotting leaves and stems, sponging up the water and releasing it only slowly, it will be ideal for a wetland garden.

I can usually assess the growing conditions of any garden after just a few minutes' observation and walking around, and you can do the same. First test the soil underfoot – if it squelches as you tread on it and water oozes out from under your boot, you have certainly got a damp garden. Squeeze a handful of the soil in your fist, and watch if water seeps out. And confirm your diagnosis by excavating a few test holes around the garden. This will keep your neighbours entertained for hours, watching your frenzy of digging, but it always reveals the secrets of soil. Make each hole about one spade deep and wide. Inspect the soil that is removed and compare it with the table on page 10, and then leave the holes overnight, to see if they fill with water.

Robust, rapid-growing plants flourish next to a permanent water source.

Next, check out the plants that are widespread and growing well in your area. Look for any of the typical wetland species (see page 84), but in particular notice if there are obvious larger moisture-loving plants such as willows, poplars, alders and dogwoods in the locality. And do not dismiss garden weeds: lawn invaders like rushes and sedges are classic indicator plants.

If all these tests prove positive, then you probably have the perfect site for a wetland garden. This is not always recognized as a blessing, and gardening books are full of advice about how to open up soils and improve drainage. This can be very relevant if you want to grow roses or runner beans, and even wetland plants may benefit from a little preliminary encouragement such as adding humus where this is lacking or opening up a channel for stagnant water to escape. But if you have a damp site and want to create a natural wetland garden, everything is in your favour.

So rejoice, and start thinking plants!

finding the ideal spot

You might think it seems ridiculous that anyone should need guidance on how to identify a damp garden. I have often been called on to provide advice on why plants are failing to flourish, however, and it is surprising how many gardeners grasp the complexities of designing a garden, but forget to consider the basics, like aspect, exposure or soil conditions.

If you are in doubt as to how to find water, my immediate suggestion would be to follow children and dogs – both seem to have a natural desire not only to seek out water but also to roll in the mud that's always associated with it! I certainly never had any trouble finding it during my childhood, and I usually managed inadvertently to bring a sample home with me, slopping around in the bottom of my wellington boots.

A little tip if this happens to you: the best method of drying out wellies that have been accidentally filled with water is to stuff them with old newspapers. Ask my mum – she had to do that to mine often enough!

cuttings

◼ **If your garden lies in a frost pocket, it should make a great wetland garden. Like water, frost flows downhill, so if frost gathers above ground, there is a good chance there will be water below.**

◼ **You can improve a wet soil that is heavily trodden and compacted by digging it over and adding grit to open up the soil structure. This will help plant roots to penetrate and establish without compromising the wet nature of the site.**

◼ **Soils high in moisture levels warm up slowly in spring, because water loses heat again more rapidly than solid mineral materials, so plants can be slow to settle down and start growing early in the season.**

◼ **It is often suggested that wet soils are infertile because the nutrients are washed out, but flowing water also brings them in, and if it comes from a mineral-rich soil it will supply many nutrients for your plants. If it flows from an impoverished soil, of course, it will bring in few foods.**

This wetland garden is as much about foliage texture and shape as it is about flower colour.

plants

of the natural wetland garden

Plants play an integral role in the natural wetland – they can hardly resist the near-perfect growing conditions! – and they are the gems in any domestic damp garden. There is a huge range of moisture-loving plants, however, and you can often find yourself spoilt for choice when it comes to selecting plants for even the most apparently hostile conditions – so there is plenty of potential for making mistakes.

The solution, of course, is provided by nature itself. Ignore the exotics and the more seasonal bog plants on sale in aquatic garden centres, and learn first from the plants that grow almost everywhere in natural wetland gardens. Look, too, at the sites they tend to occupy, and you will find that many are quite particular about where they put down their roots.

I like to think of them as falling into four broad categories, partly identified by the conditions they enjoy most, but also according to their order of arrival in the natural damp garden. The same groupings apply to the garden plants you can choose when designing wetland beds and borders, so in each group I have added some of my favourite cultivated plants that will enjoy the same conditions as their wild cousins.

the pioneers

The first to establish themselves in the wild are robust, rapid-growing plants that can thrive in conditions far too hostile for many others. They include bogbean, a pinkish white-flowered perennial with stout spreading rhizomes (see page 63), blue water speedwell, another creeping pioneer that seeds itself widely, and the familiar marsh marigold, which is happy in any kind of moist situation. They can flourish where water sits permanently in a shifting soil, because they have specially adapted fibrous roots to cope with changing water levels. Often the entire plant is submerged as the water ebbs and flows, but their whippy stems and shoots are flexible enough to avoid damage. To make matters worse, they can be subjected to intense heat, both from direct sunshine and from sunlight reflected off the surface of the water. For protection against scorching, their leaves are often thick and waxy or glossy, while some plants have cunningly reduced the exposed surface area by evolving narrow or sword-like leaves.

These tough, dependable plants are brilliant for cultivated wetland schemes, and do wonders for your confidence, for there is nothing quite like seeing a new plant settle in and grow well to spur the most cautious gardener on. One of the best to start with is *Iris fulva*. This rhizomatous iris bears coppery-red flowers on zigzagging stems up to 45cm (18in) tall, but don't be fooled by its delicate good looks – it is a sturdy survivor, and in bog gardens will need regular cutting back and division in autumn. Its common name of segg comes from the Anglo-Saxon word for sword because of its slender strap-like leaves.

To add a little vibrant sulphur-yellow to the pioneer planting scheme, you could choose *Primula florindae*, the giant cowslip from the streams and marshes of Tibet and an extrovert cousin of our own mild-mannered wild cowslip. It is a stout, eye-catching plant, with 1.2m (4ft) tall stems of pendent flowers above lush cushions of deep green leaves. An energetic spreader, it can colonize the bank of a stream almost while you have gone to make tea.

Caltha palustris var. *alba* is just as determined but more compact, although still of imposing size, and a little more demure, never becoming straggly or unruly. A slightly less familiar relative of nature's own marsh marigold, which has bright yellow buttercup-like flowers, this produces delicate single white blooms that open in spring, often before the foliage, and continue well into summer.

cuttings

■ The various sundews (*Drosera* species) are some of the stars of acid bogs. These plants compensate for the low fertility by catching and digesting insects as a nutrient supplement. Their ability to lure insects inspired early herbalists to suggest that the dew from their foliage could be used in potions to capture your true love.

■ The foliage of bog myrtle (*Myrica gale*), a suckering red-stemmed shrub, has such a pungently resinous scent that it is used to perfume candles, to enliven cooked foods in the same way as sage, and even to flavour some ales. It is used commercially as the basis of insect repellent, and in a more pure form, simply rubbing the leaves over your skin can discourage midges.

■ In some parts of the country, the white silky plumes of the common cottongrass (*Eriophorum angustifolium* – see Plants table, page 92) were gathered for stuffing pillows and, during the First World War, were used as a substitute for wound-dressings.

from left to right *Primula florindae* (giant cowslip) and *Caltha palustris* var. *alba* (a relative of the marsh marigold).

Lastly, it is always worth including a curiosity – natural gardens of all kinds are full of them! – and *Juncus effusus* 'Spiralis' is a bizarre, easily-grown rush, and certainly the only form of the wild soft rush worth growing in gardens. Each of its leafless stems is twisted into a perfect corkscrew, so that the whole plant develops into a fascinating mound of chaotic foliage. It is guaranteed to add a touch of whimsy to your garden, and looks great in a stylish modern scheme.

vigorous herbaceous plants

The next group of plants to establish themselves in wetlands enjoy full sun as much as the pioneers, and so share many of their leaf characteristics, but are a little more choosy, preferring a stable soil in which to set up home and a little less moisture at their roots.

These vigorous herbaceous species often have explosive growth rates, partly because they efficiently exploit nutrient-rich soils and partly because they multiply fast; their seeds spread widely on the wind or in the water. They are often so competitive and successful that they can become pests! The majority are dominant flowering herbaceous plants, and include hemp agrimony, a majestic riverside giant often reaching 1.5m (5ft) tall, the familiar and equally impressive yellow flag iris, and wild balsam, a 1.8m (6ft) annual with curiously hooded yellow flowers.

They all look authentic growing in the truly wild wetland garden if you have enough space, but there are plenty of other equally showy but more restrained herbaceous plants you can explore if the mood takes you.

from left to right Juncus effusus
'Spiralis' (corkscrew rush), Lythrum salicaria
(purple loosestrife), Filipendula ulmaria
(meadowsweet) and Rheum palmatum
(Chinese rhubarb).

wild balsam

If you are tempted to plant a wild balsam in your damp garden, stick to one of the native species such as the touch-me-not balsam (*Impatiens noli-tangere*), which I've already mentioned, the orange *I. capensis* or the small balsam (*I. parviflora*).

Do not be beguiled by Himalayan balsam (*I. glandulifera*) which is a huge and glamorous pink-purple annual, formerly cultivated only in gardens but now a widespread plague in the wild.

Surely the most dramatic of them all is gunnera, sometimes referred to as giant rhubarb, although that name belongs to the Chinese *Rheum palmatum*, a true rhubarb and quite massive, but no rival for this gigantic foliage plant. It is just not possible to walk past an established clump of gunnera without stopping to stare or to touch the magnificent 2m (6½ft) wide leaves, armed with fearsome spines and tall enough to shelter you from the rain. An inhabitant of tropical wetlands ever since prehistoric times, it looks a tough and ruggedly handsome monster, especially when topped with its fearsome red flower spikes, but it is in fact deciduous and slightly frost-tender, and appreciates a protective blanket of bracken or its own cut leaves over the crown to help it through a cold winter.

For something a little less dominating, there is a cultivated loosestrife that displays all the elegance of a foxtail lily (*Eremurus*), but with the added ability to cope with wet soils. *Lysimachia clethroides* is a vigorous, spreading perennial from the Far East, with rhizomatous roots, softly hairy foliage and sinuous spires of white summer flowers up to 1m (3⅓ft) high. Another species, this time a native wild plant but sufficiently well-behaved to grace any wetland area, is *L. vulgaris*, the yellow loosestrife that was once used as a fly repellent and a sedative for excitable horses. Purple loosestrife (*Lythrum salicaria*) is a brilliant reddish-purple wildflower of European marshes and a popular garden perennial.

To complete this descending canopy of plants, there is golden meadowsweet (*Filipendula ulmaria* 'Aurea'). Whereas the simple species – a lovely native flower that is sometimes known as queen of the meadows – will grow up to 1.2m (4ft), this is a little gem just 30cm (12in) tall. It makes up for lack of height

cuttings

■ Whereas downy birch revels in wet soils, its more familiar cousin, the silver birch (*Betula pendula*) prefers drier sites, although it often tolerates damp ground. Bark from all kinds of birch has a long history of being used in leather-tanning. The young twigs are still burned to flavour smoked hams and herrings, and the sap is tapped in spring to make vinegar and wine.

■ Soapwort (*Saponaria officinalis*) is a herbaceous perennial with strong woody roots and a liking for romping in the shade beneath trees and shrubs. The Romans used to make an effective soap-substitute by boiling its shoots, and its foaming properties are still used sometimes to produce a good 'head' on beer.

with its vibrant, glowing foliage that turns from bright golden yellow in spring to a soft lime green in summer. I am not a big fan of yellow foliage, particularly in a natural garden, but for me this one is the exception. Delicate and almost fern-like, its foliage is showy enough to warrant space, especially when you add its frothy display of thousands of white flowers that gently shimmer in every summer breeze.

woody plants

Trees and shrubs take time to develop their permanent woody stems, and are slower to colonize new ground, following on from the herbaceous plants and tending to occupy the comparatively drier soils further away from the water's edge. These taller, deeper-rooting plants require a firm, stable soil where they can spend several decades developing a dense, branching canopy and completing their life cycle.

Traditional trees of British natural wetlands are the elegant alder, birches such as the downy birch (*Betula pubescens*), which can cope with frequently water-logged soil, and willows, especially the crack willow, *Salix fragilis*, which you can see lining river courses throughout Europe. They all have shallower fibrous roots than most other species, and manage to avoid venturing far below the water table, staying relatively near the surface and helping to bind the soil together.

In your own wetland garden, woody plants will provide structure and shade, and the classic tree and shrub genus for waterside planting is willow or *Salix*, a name derived quite simply from the Celtic words *sal*, meaning near, and *lis*, which is water. It is an important group of trees with great claim to medical fame

because it is used for the production of salicylic acid, refined in 1899 to produce aspirin.

My favourite among them is the wonderful orange-stemmed *Salix alba* subsp. *vitellina* 'Britzensis', the scarlet or coral-barked willow that used to be called 'Chermesina'. It creates dappled shade from a flowing canopy of long branches, and can become quite a sizeable medium tree that might be a little boisterous and unmanageable for some gardens, unless you coppice it every couple of years, which will enhance the colour of its bare stems in winter (see page 99).

If you are not afraid of height and are searching for a tree to make an architectural statement, the dawn redwood might be the perfect choice, as unforgettable as its Latin name, *Metasequoia glyptostroboides*. This conifer, one of only a few deciduous kinds, is a slender 18m (60ft) cone of soft blue-green needles on elegant drooping stems, and looks simply stunning, especially in autumn when it lights up with brilliant brick- and ruby-red tints. It is a tough tree once established, although it grows best where summers are generally hot and the soils very moist, showing a remarkable ability to survive even when the roots are entirely submerged in water.

Some plants are a top choice because of their foliage, others for their flowers, but in the woody category there are some amazing shrubs worth growing just for their stems. Two of my favourites for a wetland site are several kinds of *Cornus*, or dogwood, and the golden or fishpole bamboo (*Phyllostachys aurea*) which is botanically a grass but is treated more like a shrub in garden design terms. One of the most vivid varieties of the red-barked dogwood (*Cornus alba*) is the variety 'Sibirica', which used to be called 'Westonbirt'. It is an elegant shrub that will sit

from left to right *Betula pubescens* (downy birch), *Salix alba* (white willow), *Metasequoia glyptostroboides* (dawn redwood), *Phyllostachys aurea* (golden bamboo) and *Cornus alba* (red-barked dogwood).

there quietly all summer, modestly allowing other plants to grab your attention. But as winter approaches and its reddening leaves fall, you are greeted by the most stunning, gleaming coral-crimson stems. Their brilliant colour is even more intense on the youngest stems so it pays to coppice this one regularly. Golden bamboo behaves quite differently, producing its outstanding sunny stems along with its evergreen golden green foliage. Unlike the branches of dogwoods, bamboo needs time to evolve its best colour, and only when mature do the stems turn from a juvenile dowdy green to a gorgeous golden brown.

the ground layer

Finally, down near the surface, we find the last group of plants, the shade-loving species that can be rapid in growth, and revel in the damp soils of the water margins. These are the broad-leaved or feathery herbaceous plants such as bugle, and the royal and marsh ferns, whose foliage is delicate in structure but expansive enough to absorb most of the dappled light available under the canopy of the deciduous trees. Keep them constantly moist and protect them from scorching in the sun, and they will dominate the ground layer with their delightful foliage. They need to nestle in the very heart of the damp garden ecosystem, cradled in shade, moisture and humidity.

My suggestions for gardens must include my favourite group, ferns. These are supreme foliage plants with an enormous range of variation, because the intricately cut fronds of many kinds will often differ in some of their details. In

from left to right *Matteuccia struthiopteris* (ostrich-feather or shuttlecock fern), *Ajuga reptans* (bugle) and *Luzula nivea* (snowy woodrush).

isolation this might look insignificant, but it can be enough to give the whole plant a quite distinct appearance and, eventually, a new name.

Some ferns thrive in dry, even sunny positions, but most prefer cool, moist shade, and there is such a vast choice of these that it is only possible to recommend a couple. The common names of *Matteuccia struthiopteris* – the ostrich-feather or shuttlecock fern – between them describe exactly how it looks. Its neatly divided, deciduous fronds, 1–1.2m (3⅓–4ft) long or more, stand erect and cluster in an immaculate ring, like a perfect vase or shuttlecock, making it without doubt the most elegant of all ferns. Its creeping horizontal rhizomes spread efficiently, so keep a close eye on its progress if space is short.

You should certainly not let it swamp more timid ferns such as *Polystichum setiferum*, which normally only grows 60cm (2ft) high, although in fertile, humus-rich soil it can reach almost 1.2m (4ft). It has the advantage of being evergreen, and so it will keep its softly arching, rich green fronds over the winter, unless excessively heavy rainfall disfigures them. It prefers slightly better-drained soils than those that the shuttlecock fern enjoys, and may not grow so well in the very wettest ground.

In case you think I am biased towards ferns, let me recommend adding *Luzula nivea* to the shaded ground layer. This is the evergreen snowy woodrush, just 30cm (12in) high and fairly slow to grow and spread into loose tussocks. Be patient though, because it is worth waiting to enjoy its dense clusters of shining white flower spikes in early summer as they add little glimmers of light to the lush green understorey.

fabulous ferns

One popular fern, the adder's-tongue (*Ophioglossum vulgatum*), was, by association, believed in medieval times to be a cure for snake bites because the characteristic shape of its annual single frond looks very like the tongue of a snake.

The curious thing about ferns generally is that their propagation was only discovered in 1794, when botanists finally tried to identify and explain the spores on the back of the fronds. This was many years after they had become well-established as ornamental plants.

You can grow hardy ferns, whether single species or in mixtures, simply by scattering the spores on the surface of a tray of wet, soilless compost – do not bury them. Cover the tray with a clear lid to keep the contents moist, and stand it in a warm place indoors, away from the sun.

At first you will see flat, leaf-like discs appear on the surface and these develop cup- or stalk-like protuberances as they fertilize each other. Finally the ferns will emerge and can be potted up when large enough to handle.

plants for a wetland garden

the pioneers

Glyceria maxima var. variegata
(syn. *G. aquatica variegata, G. spectabilis* 'Variegata')
reed sweet grass
height 75–80cm (30–32in).
spread Indefinite.
habit Hardy deciduous perennial grass with spreading rhizomes.
season Foliage spring–autumn; flowers July–August.
site Full sun or very light shade, in boggy soil and water to 20cm (8in) or deeper.
characteristics Arching sword-shaped creamy-white leaves with green edges flushed pink in spring, and branching spikes of greenish purple flowers. Spreads rapidly into dense clumps.
how to grow Sow or plant in spring 30–45cm (12–18in) apart, in wet soil or in baskets to limit spread. Cut down and clear dead foliage in late autumn, or leave in place in a wild garden.

Veronica beccabunga
brooklime
height 10–15cm (4–6in).
spread Indefinite.
habit Hardy evergreen or semi-evergreen perennial, with creeping stems.
season Flowers May–August/September.
site Full sun or light shade, in boggy soil and water to 10cm (4in) deep.
characteristics Rounded, fleshy leaves (once picked for spring salads) and loose heads of vivid blue flowers, each with a white eye. Its sprawling stems spread rapidly, rooting where they touch the soil and making excellent ground cover.
how to grow Sow or plant in spring, 30cm (12in) apart, in the soil or confined in baskets.
note Despite its name, this is not confined to alkaline soils – 'lime' comes from an Anglo-Saxon word simply meaning 'plant'.

Eriophorum angustifolium
common or narrow-leaved cottongrass
height 30–45cm (12–18in).
spread 75cm (30in).
habit Hardy evergreen perennial sedge, with long creeping rhizomes.
season Flowers April–May; seed heads May–July.
site Full sun or very light shade, in damp or boggy acid soils and water to 5cm (2in) deep.
characteristics Long fine-textured drooping leaves and small spikes of tiny yellow-centred flowers, followed by brown seed pods wrapped in silky white plumes like loose cotton buds. A tough plant, spreading rapidly into large drifts of tight clumps.
how to grow Sow or plant in spring 30cm (12in) apart. Mulch with compost in spring until established.
note The broad-leaved cottongrass (*E. latifolium*) is similar, but prefers alkaline soils.

vigorous herbaceous plants

Zantedeschia aethiopica
arum or calla lily
height 90cm (3ft).
spread 60cm (2ft).
habit Fairly hardy herbaceous perennial, with slowly creeping rhizomes.
season Flowers May–August.
site Full sun, in wet fertile soils and water to 30cm (12in) deep.
characteristics Deep green, glossy leaves, broad and arrow-shaped, and tiny yellow flowers clustered on a spike surrounded by a large and exotic, pure white spathe. Spreads into lush, boldly textured clumps.
how to grow Plant in spring 45cm (18in) apart, in groups. Mulch dormant plants with leaves where winter temperatures regularly fall below -5°C (23°F).
note The variety 'Crowborough' has larger spathes and is hardier than the species.

Darmera peltata
(syn. *Peltiphyllum peltatum*)
umbrella weed or plant
height 1.8m (6ft).
spread 90cm (3ft).
habit Hardy herbaceous perennial, with vigorously spreading rhizomes.
season Flowers April–May; autumn leaf tints August–November.
site Full sun or light shade, in moist or boggy soil.
characteristics Fat heads of star-shaped pink flowers, followed by dense clumps of broad rounded leaves like a huge, deeply textured saxifrage. Dark green for most of the season, these turn coppery red in autumn.
how to grow Sow or plant in spring, 45cm (18in) apart in small groups. Feed and mulch with compost in spring.
note The dwarf form 'Nana' is half this size, and a better choice for small gardens.

Lysichiton camtschatcensis
white skunk cabbage
height 75cm (30in).
spread 75cm (30in).
habit Hardy herbaceous perennial with short spreading rhizomes.
season Flowers March–April.
site Full sun or light shade in deep rich wet soil and water up to 10cm (4in) deep.
characteristics Dense clumps of coarse light green foliage, almost prehistoric in appearance, and spectacular bold arum-like spathes up to 40cm (16in) long with an unusual musky scent.
how to grow Plant in spring 75cm (30in) apart. Feed in spring and, in very cold gardens, mulch over winter.
note The yellow skunk cabbage (*L. americanus*) is even larger and smellier, with brilliant yellow spathes.

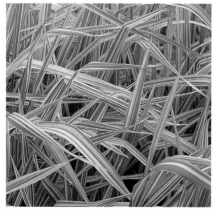
Glyceria maxima var. *variegata* (reed sweet grass)

Veronica beccabunga (brooklime)

Eriophorum angustifolium (common or narrow-leaved cottongrass)

woody plants

ground layer plants

Alnus glutinosa 'Imperialis'

cut-leaved alder

height 6m (20ft).

spread 3m (10ft).

habit Hardy deciduous tree with conical upright growth.

season Catkins February–March; foliage April–October.

site Full sun or light shade, in any wet soil.

characteristics An elegant slender tree, ideal for small gardens, with an upright branching canopy of finely cut foliage. The long pendent catkins appear early, before the leaves, and are followed in mid-summer by round 'cones' that turn brown and last all winter.

how to grow Plant in winter or spring, and stake and mulch for the first 3–4 years. If necessary, prune to shape in early winter.

note Alders coppice well and the cut wood can be turned into high quality charcoal.

Sorbaria kirilowii

(syn. *Spiraea arborea*) bog spiraea

height 6–8m (20–26ft).

width 6m (20ft).

habit Hardy deciduous suckering shrub.

season Foliage spring–autumn; flowers July–August.

site Full sun or partial shade, in moist neutral or alkaline soil.

characteristics A robust, suckering shrub, forming thickets of vigorous arching growth, with elegant fern-like foliage and long spires of foaming white flowers. A good tough plant for informal gardens.

how to grow Plant in autumn or winter, and prune hard after planting. Prune annually in winter and remove some of the suckers to limit height and spread.

note *S. sorbifolia* is similar but smaller in all respects.

Populus tremula

common aspen

height 20m (65ft).

spread 10m (33ft).

habit Hardy deciduous medium-sized tree or large suckering shrub.

season Catkins February–March; foliage tints autumn.

site Full sun, in any wet soil.

characteristics A fast-growing upright tree with an airy pyramidal canopy. Long greyish red catkins drape the whole tree before the appearance of the delicate leaves, which shimmer and tremble in every breeze and turn a stunning clear yellow in autumn.

how to grow Plant in winter or spring, and stake and mulch for the first 3–4 years. Can be pruned in winter to limit size.

note Aspens have a reputation for forecasting rain, possibly because their leaves rustle loudly in the breeze that precedes a shower.

Aronia x prunifolia

purple chokeberry

height 3m (10ft).

spread 2.4m (8ft).

habit Hardy deciduous suckering shrub.

season Flowers May; berries and leaf tints autumn.

site Full sun or dappled shade, on moist neutral or acid soils.

characteristics A medium-sized upright shrub with hairy deep green leaves that turn fiery orange-purple in autumn. The white pink-tinged flowers, like those of hawthorn, are followed by conspicuous purple-black berries.

how to grow Plant in winter or spring. Prune out suckers and some of the older shoots in winter.

note The variety 'Brilliant' has vivid red autumn tints.

Gaultheria shallon

shallon or salal

height 1.2m (4ft).

spread 1.5m (5ft).

habit Hardy evergreen suckering shrub, with spreading underground stems.

season Flowers May–June; berries autumn/winter.

site Dappled shade, in moist acid soils rich in humus.

characteristics A tough and vigorous rounded shrub that makes an excellent thicket of ground cover in shady places. It has lush leathery leaves, dark green with reddish tints in winter, and white bell-like flowers followed by large clusters of deep purple berries.

how to grow Plant in autumn or spring. Chop off unwanted suckers in spring with a spade.

note The checkerberry (*G. procumbens*), its cousin, creeps along the ground 45cm (18in) high and bears scarlet berries.

Liriope muscari

lily turf

height 30cm (12in).

spread 45cm (18in).

habit Hardy evergreen or semi-evergreen tuberous perennial.

season Flowers September–November.

site Dappled or full shade, sheltered from cold winds, in moist neutral or slightly acid soils.

characteristics Densely tufted grassy clumps of lush dark green strap-like foliage and luxuriant crowded spikes of bright lilac flowers in autumn. A good colonizer for wet shrubby and woodland areas.

how to grow Plant in spring, 30cm (12in) apart in small groups. Lift and divide every 4–5 years if it becomes invasive.

note There are many named varieties in white and various shades of blue, and also variegated kinds.

Zantedeschia aethiopica (arum or calla lily)

Alnus glutinosa 'Imperialis' (cut-leaved alder)

Gaultheria shallon (shallon or salal)

a season

in the natural wetland garden

Looking after a wetland garden is always a pleasure and comparatively undemanding, provided you remember it is possible to inadvertently do more damage than good by trampling the ground as you tend the plants. The soil structure in a water-logged garden is very delicate, and every footfall can crush the life out of it, reducing the vital air gaps within the soil and forcing its particles to bond together in solid clods. These do not easily break down again and the air, already a precious commodity in moist soil, cannot be easily reintroduced (see cuttings on page 83).

The simplest way to protect your soil from compaction is to lay wooden boards over the ground when you are working in a wet area, so that your weight is more evenly distributed. Alternatively, include plenty of stepping stones and permanent paths in your design, and stay on these wherever possible, keeping a couple of boards handy to stand on when you work on the areas in between.

spring

mulching – A very wet garden, with water flowing through the site, receives a constant supply of nutrients, although the same water that feeds the ground is also responsible for removing some of the soluble foods. To correct any imbalance it is a good idea to spread an organic top-dressing over the surface of the whole wetland area once a year during the spring.

Bulky organic materials such as a loose friable mixture of partially rotted leaf-mould or garden compost are the perfect panacea for a damp garden, for several reasons. They are full of nutrients, which are released slowly as they decompose into the soil below. If you spread a layer at least 5cm (2in) deep, it will act as a blanket and reduce the loss of moisture. And the soil structure is greatly improved by the addition of organic matter, encouraging worms and

micro-organisms that carry the rotting material down into the soil, improving its friable quality and ability to retain moisture and nutrients.

A word or two of warning though – do not be tempted to make a mulch out of conifer needles because the resulting mix will be dense and have an acid pH, which can be harmful to a lot of your plants. And when you are spreading the mulch, avoid heaping the material up around the crowns of herbaceous plants, as it can be rather rich and may burn young leaves.

feeding – As we have already seen, many nutrients are carried into the wetland garden by flowing water, and you will have supplied more in the surface mulch of organic materials. As a rule, supplementary feeding with fertilizers is unnecessary and can actually cause harm if these dissolve and get carried into a pond, where they may cause a green algal bloom.

New plants, however, benefit from a light feed in their first season while they are settling in. The type of fertilizer to use is a slow-release organic feed such as bonemeal, rather than a concentrated chemical feed like Growmore. Just sprinkle a small handful round the plant and leave to break down and dissolve slowly.

planting – Spring is a good time to introduce new plants, when the soil and water are beginning to warm up and plant growth is really under way. Add plenty of organic matter when preparing the planting hole, forking it in as evenly as possible – this can be squidgy work on really wet soils, but is well worth the discomfort. Stake trees securely and trim new shrubs lightly to encourage them to bush out.

Ferns, irises and candelabra primula are an ideal planting trio for wetland areas with the delicate flowers providing colour and height amongst the dense, lush foliage of the ferns.

A highlight of white foliage and sprays
of creamy flowers make a perfect accent
to intense green.

With herbaceous plants, arrange several in a natural group, planting them fairly close together so that each will help support its neighbour. This reduces the need to provide canes or wire hoops for additional support, and there will be less bare ground in between for weeds to creep in and colonize, which means in turn that you will not have to tread on the soil so often to tend your plants.

propagation – This is an essential part of spring maintenance. Vigorous and long-established herbaceous plants eventually need lifting and dividing into smaller, younger portions, which you can transplant to new positions elsewhere or, very often, replant in the same place after refreshing the soil with compost and a little bonemeal. Always keep the outer segments of clumps for replanting, as these are the youngest and most energetic, and discard the older central portions.

Many natural wetland species can be introduced into your garden by sowing them now, or in early autumn if you have access to fresh seeds. Sow them in trays of moist compost in a cool greenhouse or cold frame and make sure they never dry out, or prepare a corner of the wetland garden as a nursery bed and sow them in rows there. Transplant or thin the seedlings when you can handle them comfortably, spacing them about 5–8cm (2–3in) apart, and leave to grow on until large enough to plant out in their permanent positions.

summer

watering – This is the time of year when you might have little to do in the wetland garden, apart from enjoying its unique environment. Your plants will be growing lavishly and, as they come into flower, will usually attract a host of specialized wildlife. Toads, frogs and newts laze in the damp shade now their season of courtship and spawning is over, dragonflies search any wet spot for egg-laying sites, and if you have tall grasses or sedges you might even get a reed warbler singing from its camouflaged perch.

In a very dry summer, when everywhere else is gasping for water and showing signs of stress, the wetland garden will be a cool and refreshing green oasis, where the plants thrive unchecked as they continue drawing on the huge reserves of stored ground water. In fact, you might not think moisture loss could ever be a problem in a damp garden, but even here mid-summer heat can reduce soil water levels so that naturally damp-loving plants are faced with conditions that are far too arid for them to thrive happily.

Topping up water levels in the wetland garden as a whole is not a practical proposition – we are talking huge volumes of water – but you may need to help new young plants along as they try to get established. Give them a good individual soaking during the evening. Allow a canful or two of water to each plant or leave a hosepipe gently trickling for an hour beside a young tree or shrub. Then mulch thickly to prevent the soil from drying out again too fast.

controlling growth – Of course, creating an environment where each plant has a home that is perfect for its needs can cause problems if they then thrive so successfully that they become invasive. It is important to police the garden with some firmness, especially now when most of the plants are growing flat out and

cuttings

■ The pretty lilac-pink *Althaea officinalis* or marsh mallow was the original source of the sickly sweet confectionery of the same name. Marshmallows used to be made by infusing the fresh roots (rich in sugar, starch and gelatinous oils), in water, or by cooking the powdered root with sugar.

■ Medieval herbalists believed that chewing the dried flowers or roots of meadowsweet (*Filipendula ulmaria*) could cure fevers and headaches. Unlike many old wives' tales, there is some foundation for this because the flower buds actually contain salicylic acid, from which aspirin was synthesized.

■ The purple-flowered stinking iris or roast beef plant (*Iris foetidissima*) is a common sight in the wild on moist shaded alkaline soils. It gets its popular name from the strong smell of meat given off by the crushed foliage.

With careful planning and choice of plants, the onset of autumn can bring with it a dazzling display of gold and russet.

jostling for space. Keep an eye on each group and don't be afraid to remove part of a plant if it oversteps the mark. Irises and willows can quickly become weeds if they are not monitored, and you may need to chop out a sucker or outer portion of a fat clump with your spade to restrain over-enthusiastic growth.

If you have enough meadowsweet or marsh mallow in the garden, deadhead such plants as their blooms go over to prevent further seeding. Don't do this to *Iris foetidissima* though, because its split capsules of orange seeds are part of its attraction. Instead, thin out some of the spreading rhizomes of this and other irises after flowering, and transplant them elsewhere or give them away.

autumn

clearing – Once herbaceous plants have finished flowering, it can be tempting to remove all their dead and dying top growth to make neat clumps for a tidy appearance over winter. Although this was a traditional part of the autumn border routine, it is far better to leave these dead stems in place, since removing them does more harm than good. They are a rich source of food for wildlife and provide a number of species with shelter and safety, including beneficial insects such as lacewings, which overwinter in hollow dead stems. Removing them can damage a plant too, leaving small cavities that reach right into the heart of its dormant crown, exposing this to frost and rising water levels, which can penetrate into the very core of the plant and cause problems with rot. So delay clearing dead top growth until the end of winter, even if the plants do look a little untidy. It is a *natural* wetland garden after all.

protection – Leaving old woody top growth in place can often prevent lethal frost damage to species of borderline hardiness. The foliage of herbaceous plants such as skunk cabbages, gunnera and arum lilies disintegrates almost to nothing in winter, and to protect these from frost you need to cover the dormant crowns with a layer of coarse organic material such as leaf-mould, bracken or straw. Leave this in place until after the last severe frosts. If water levels tend to rise, you can prevent this winter cover from being washed away by holding it in place with a square of wire or plastic netting, pegged or weighted down at the corners.

winter

pruning – The woody plants that provide cool shade to the wetland environment usually require the least maintenance of all your plants. Winter is the time to check them for size and shape, and if you have doubts about whether they are growing too large, you can prune or coppice them now without compromising your overall planting scheme. Remember, this is a natural garden where intervention is kept to an essential minimum, and any pruning you do needs to be restrained and subtle. Resist the temptation to clip an over-large shrub like a hedge, and instead simply remove up to one-third of the oldest branches to keep it young and vigorous, perhaps shortening one or two others at the same time to balance up the shape.

Cutting out or shortening a branch or two may be enough to reduce a tree's size to more acceptable proportions, but the traditional way to manage multi-stemmed trees of rapid growth, such as willows, is to coppice them every 3–5 years. This involves cutting all the branches to ground level or just above. In woodlands, whole areas or 'coups' are coppiced in rotation, but to avoid changing the appearance of the wetland garden too drastically, it is best to coppice just one or two trees per winter on a rota system, otherwise the canopy will be rather bare for a few years. Most deciduous trees native to British wetlands can be coppiced and seem to thrive all the better for this hard pruning, their fresh young growth making an attracive feature, especially on willows and dogwoods grown for their decorative coloured stems.

Whilst winter may lay many plants bare, the reflective quality of the water keeps the scheme alive.

the natural

Meadows are one of the most varied and diverse habitats in Britain. They are in fact gigantic herbaceous borders, stuffed with grasses and flowering plants and can easily be translated into a domestic garden, bringing to it a touch of romance.

meadow garden

origins

of the natural meadow garden

opposite Meadow plants are some of our most opportunistic – here they are thriving at the edge of a crop field.
below Sweet-smelling grass and an abundance of flowers are the epitome of meadow gardens.

A meadow is one of the most evocative and appealing of all the natural gardens. Its expanse of animated grasses, delicate flowering annuals and often imposing perennials can evoke a joyous sense of liberation – there are no paths to follow, just acres of grass and wild flowers to explore under the wide open sky.

However, meadows are much more than just romantic ideals, childhood memories of freedom and play or, if you are cynical, simply an excuse for lazy gardeners to mow only twice a year. With their huge and cosmopolitan grass-and-flower communities, they offer some of the most diverse and varied

habitats in the countryside, and some of the most colourful. Although meadow flowers may be small individually, en masse their effect can be spectacular, and instead of disparaging them as little more than elaborate lawns, we should appreciate meadows for what they really are: gigantic herbaceous borders.

They are also among the most important wild habitats, offering ideal homes to a number of specialized and precariously placed animals, plants and invertebrates, and are themselves constantly endangered by a range of serious threats: house- and road-building, changes in water levels, agricultural improvement, or simply neglect and misunderstanding of the kind of management needed to preserve their fragile eco-systems.

A meadow is strictly an area of grassland that is mown for hay, but the term is loosely used for any kind of grassland, including pasture, which is specifically grazing for farm animals. Few meadows are truly natural, and most owe their existence entirely to man's destruction of native woodlands. There are a few examples of grassland as a natural form of vegetation, but these tend to occur on very dry soils or at high levels where trees do not grow easily, and even these are grazed by wild animals. Elsewhere, grassland is an artefact, produced by clearing woods and maintained by grazing or mowing to prevent trees from returning.

From Neolithic times onwards, forests were felled for their timber, which was used as fuel and building material, and the cleared land was then utilized for animal grazing and field crops. Fire played a part in the clearance too, and was one of the main ways Indian tribes kept the North American prairies open for huge herds of buffalo to graze. The buffalo are gone now, and trees are beginning to return on the fringes of these huge artificial grasslands.

The first use of many of these cleared areas seems to have been crop cultivation, but very often the soils left after clearance were too impoverished to produce good yields or were quickly exhausted, and so were left to the only plants that could tolerate relatively infertile conditions – grasses. As a result hay meadows and pastureland developed, producing food for cattle. This also occurred in flood plains where the earth was too damp for conventional crops, but not for numerous grass and wild flower species that were able to colonize the ground and multiply, producing excellent grazing during the summer when the earth was drier and more accessible for cattle.

The continued success and survival of meadows is due entirely to this constant simple agricultural process. Whether the grass is trimmed by grazing or cut by machinery, the effects are the same: fine meadow grasses and their associated flowers thrive in those specialized conditions where their roots have little more than a shallow layer of poor soil and their top growth is constantly cut. Woody plants cannot survive the constant damage and check to growth

cuttings

■ One old custom relating to meadows was widespread years ago in Nottinghamshire, where a piece of grassland full of flowers would be dug up in summer and displayed in the house as an ornament called a 'mid-summer cushion'.

■ The ox-eye daisy or wild marguerite is one of the first wild flowers to colonize a bare patch of earth, germinating in only 2–3 weeks after sowing. It is also known as the moon daisy, because its pure white blooms appear to glow in the mid-summer moonlight.

field of dreams

On those summer days we all remember, when the sky was purest blue and the sun so hot that even boisterous lads just wanted to sit still, my brother and I would trample nests for ourselves in a Worcestershire meadow near my parents' house. Lying on our backs, with the feathery grass and wild flowers waving gently in and out of vision, we could trace the energetic flight paths of skylarks as they dashed from one horizon to another.

This might paint a rosy and very selective picture of a typically English meadow, but I'm not alone in my cherished recollections. Meadows always seemed to be precious, unchanging places of escape, but there was a more mundane, practical aspect that we ignored or knew nothing about. They didn't just happen – that meadow of ours was an important and increasingly threatened element on someone's working farm.

Now meadows have another role, and a more promising future. In the same way as denim was noticed and elevated from purely functional working-class clothing to the trendiest of fashion wear, so meadows have been transformed from barren cleared land unsuitable for anything other than rough grazing, through a golden age of pastoral stability into the most exciting of gardening styles.

inflicted by frequent cutting and are unable to move in, so the the natural succession from grassland to scrub and shrub is effectively halted.

Under this system, fertility levels stay generally low. With the soil impoverished to start with and routine management removing any top growth that might otherwise rot down and improve the soil, a wide range of undemanding plant species can live together in a delicate harmony, fed only by the dung of grazing animals. This kind of habitat can only survive while the management processes that brought about their existence in the first place continue to be followed. Grassland improvement, for example, which involves spreading heavy doses of artificial fertilizer, destroys the original balance by encouraging coarser plants, especially tough grasses, at the expense of other species.

Consequently meadows are a vulnerable and unstable feature of our landscape. Wherever mowing and grazing has ceased, scrub quickly invades, forming thickets of woody stems that exclude light and suppress the rich meadow flora. During the Second World War thousands of acres of formerly permanent meadowland and pasture were ploughed up for crop production, reluctantly in many cases because farmers knew they were a precious resource that could not be created overnight. It can take decades for the rare meadow plants to return naturally, especially as they have to compete with vigorous tussocky grasses still benefiting from remnants of fertilizers and weedkillers applied many years before.

Meadows have had their supporters, however, and it's not only small boys like I once was who have been lured by their irresistible fascination. The delicate blooms of their typical flowers have long been admired by horticulturists, and through careful selection and breeding cultivated versions have been produced to fill our borders – many kinds of cranesbill, scabious, saxifrage and annual chrysanthemum owe their origin to wild meadow species. One influential designer who greatly admired the informality of the meadow and its associated plants was Gertrude Jekyll, a name synonymous with powerful exploding borders filled to the brim with bloom after bloom. Using the natural meadow as a template, she blended colours in intricate and subtle ways that brought many of these wildflowers into mainstream gardening.

Unfortunately the grasses typical of old meadows were not revered with quite the same enthusiasm as the flowers, and so they remained relegated to the fields and verges. Ironically, I feel it is the original blend of flowers and grasses that is the key to the kind of emotional response meadows evoke. A planting scheme that concentrates solely on highly cultivated and coloured blooms ignores that unfathomable and slightly romantic charm, the very essence of meadows that captivated Jekyll in the first place.

In North America, the prairie – the US equivalent of the meadow – also started something of a garden trend for the same reasons. Prairies have almost iconic status in American history and affections, but have been threatened by development and agriculture in the same way as English meadows. They are characterized by the same mix of annuals, perennials and grasses, except that everything is much bigger, and not just because of the difference in scale. Prairie soils are rich and fertile, with a nutrient-rich base which sustains plants that can grow to gargantuan proportions, often well over 1.8m (6ft) in height. Concern over the loss of this diverse flora encouraged planting schemes in parks of native grasses and perennials such as eupatorium, echinacea and golden rod, and these ideas have been taken up in private gardens as an alternative to extensive mown lawns.

On both sides of the Atlantic an increasingly rare historical landscape feature has achieved recognition just in time and, as often happens, it is the ordinary back garden that could be the best sanctuary for this natural habitat.

Nature has no inhibitions, mixing colours from scarlet through purple and pink to cooling white.

identifying
the potential meadow garden

Both the English meadow and the American prairie are natural environments that have an undoubted appeal, but neither appear altogether suitable for a domestic garden. For a start they are large-scale features that depend on agricultural practices alien to traditional gardening skills. Furthermore, garden soils are comparatively rich in nutrients, whereas native meadow plants specialize in surviving on poor soils and would be out-competed by more vigorous plants.

   American experience with handling plants that require far more space than most of us have, however, has resulted in a hybrid style in which a framework of

fine-leaved grasses add movement, texture and structure while vigorous cultivated perennials and annuals provide flowering drama, all in a combination that
is then scaled down to suit the back garden. Couple this with a simplified maintenance regime, and you have a unique planting style that is highly attractive to
the contemporary gardener. In this country ecologists have led the way in creating or repairing meadows along similar lines, concentrating decades of slow
evolution into a few years of carefully planned restoration.

Think back to that childhood memory of lying carefree in a meadow. It shows
us straightaway one of the environmental conditions essential for successfully
creating a garden version: bright blue sky and no shade from the summer sun.
All meadow plants are sun-lovers and thrive in areas where the tree canopy –
and, therefore, any overhead shade – has been eliminated. There is no chance
of competition from intrusive woody plants either, because the constant cropping regime ensures they have no chance of invading. So in your garden you
first need to find a site where the same conditions apply, avoiding all areas
under or near trees and large shrubs, and free even from shadows cast by
buildings or walls.

Do not worry too much about the soil. A typical meadow might have thin poor
soil, but in a garden context you have to accept what you have got – it is much

A carpet of flowers and grasses
captivates gardeners, but for the mammals
and insects it is even more enticing.

Cooling green is the perfect foil for these vibrant blooms. Without the grass this collection of flowers would seem garish.

easier to improve soil than to exhaust existing fertility! American prairies are filled with the greediest of plants, luxuriating in soil that is high in nutrients and organic matter, and able to hold the moisture they need for lavish growth. In fact, prairie conditions are very similar to those of most domestic gardens, favouring the rapid establishment of grasses and wild flowers. Some will certainly grow too vigorously and threaten to take over, but occasional selective interference on your part can control them while favouring less competitive species, and if you make a point of removing all the top growth you cut down annually, the soil will gradually decline in fertility.

The site of my first prairie scheme was in my parents' garden, in a vegetable patch that had been abandoned as surplus to needs. Like all good veg plots it was in full sun, and years of constant double digging and manuring had left the ground rich and friable, far more fertile than, say, the thin poor soil of the chalk downs. There the meadow flowers, although individually exquisite, are usually tiny, reflecting the meagre nutrients and moisture available to them. But they do not need to look sparse and starved, as my kitchen-garden prairie revealed with its drifts of graceful grasses and sheets of colour.

Far more important is your garden's acidity and drainage. There are few soils that will not support a meadow of some kind and many wild flowers can be grown on acid ground, but the widest and most colourful range enjoy alkaline conditions, with a pH of 6.5–7.0. Test the chosen site with a simple bought kit, and if the results show a reading much lower than this, apply a dressing of lime (the kit will tell you how much) or, better, calcified seaweed for longer-term benefits such as the slow release of trace elements. Check, too, whether the plants you want to grow prefer heavy or light ground. There are species for every situation, even heavy wet clay which would be ideal for water-meadow flora, but you may need to add humus to light soils or dig and aerate heavy ground for certain favourite species.

Once you have identified and selected the site for your natural meadow garden, you need to decide how to set about creating it. In the natural course of events, grasses and annuals would move in first, establishing a thin, changing cover of vegetation with bare spaces that are gradually colonized by slower-growing perennials. But many gardeners prefer to sow a complete wild flower meadow mixture on bare ground and leave the various ingredients to jostle for space and supremacy until they settle down as a stable community. This is a useful option, especially as prepared mixtures are available for all kinds of soil and habitat, from dry chalk to acid wetland, and also to provide flowers in particular seasons.

If you are really daring, you might decide to turn your lawn – or part of it, at least – into a wild flower meadow, especially if you have been less than conscientious about keeping it weed-free and well-fed. A lawn that is patchy and already infiltrated by low-growing plants such as dandelions, daisies and tiny blue speedwell has a head start over a lush bowling green, which may be too rich and would be best stripped of turf and topsoil to remove all that accumulated fertility. On a poor lawn, all you need do is raise the mower's cutting height in areas you select as paths and abandon mowing the rest until July, if you want a spring meadow, or mow up to then for a later display. Spot-plant additional species or sow wild flower seed in the bare patches.

In a border you can sow a prepared mixture or a packet each of several chosen species, or you could follow the more traditional gardening approach by planting specimens and groups of clump-forming grasses and perennials, which you leave to grow and seed freely and then cut down at the end of winter. Among them you can sow annuals, allowing these to seed themselves too. Purists will say that you should remove all the top growth so that nothing is returned to the soil and fertility levels decline, but a counsel of perfection for an authentic wild flower meadow is probably too rigorous for a border of meadow plants where a more lavish display is appropriate. I would suggest you compost the cleared growth, and then return this or a dressing of well-rotted manure as a spring mulch around plants.

plants

of the natural meadow garden

Selecting plants for the natural meadow garden, whether it is a liberated lawn or a carefully composed border, is probably harder than stocking any other kind of natural garden and is not a task for the faint-hearted. For a start the range is enormous, even after you exclude species like wild orchids and parasitic plants that will not grow well in domestication, together with all those wild flowers more familiar as weeds of cultivated ground: nettles, thistles, ground elder, Japanese knotweed and all their undesirable allies. That still leaves plenty to go on with.

You also need every ounce of bravery to tear up the rule book and throw out long-established principles of subtly blending one shade of colour with another. Don't even think of compartmentalizing colours, for this is gardening without inhibitions. The effect you need to aim for is an untamed riot of colour, texture and form, and that means mixing reds and oranges, say, with blue and pink. The border might seem a complex and vibrant mix of clashing colours, but you will find that individual plants come into their own at different times of day: when the sun at its height, for example, the brilliant yellows of rudbeckias will glow with colour, but in the evening light the calming blues of salvias and scabious will take over. And with this scheme, there are plenty of plants to choose from.

the grasses

Anyone who has ever weeded a border will not be surprised to learn that the first plants to move in on freshly cleared land are the grasses. In many ways they are the ultimate pioneers, able to distribute thousands of light airborne seeds every season and starting to colonize bare spaces before the flowering plants are out of bed.

They are essential to any wild meadow community and tend to dominate, partly because (unlike other plants) they grow from the base of the leaf not the tip of a shoot and therefore are able to withstand constant cutting. Even in a small and ungrazed garden border they have a purpose. Limiting your planting to wild flowers might give you more colour than you ever dreamed of, but these action plants would be nothing without grasses, whose unique form is an indispensable ingredient of any composition, their subtle greens and bronzes and the constant movement of their insubstantial foliage making a soothing foil to the clashing colours of the flowers.

The grass you are probably most likely to meet in a meadow is *Poa annua*, appropriately called the annual meadowgrass, and it often pops up around the garden as a seedling from the lawn. Almost worldwide in its spread, it is a relatively insubstantial species but, like most grasses, quite beautiful when you look at it closely, especially when its dainty branching flower-head appears. It grows fast and can flower at almost any time of year, quickly seeding and spreading to cracks in paths and anywhere else that it can find a tiny niche. It is too soft and flimsy for meadow or border use, but it has a fine perennial cousin, *P. glauca* or glaucous meadowgrass, which is a mountain species often cultivated for the ornamental bluish-white bloom on all its parts.

Most of the more persistent grasses in a meadow are perennial, surviving and spreading indefinitely by sprouting new shoots from their underground rhizomes. As anyone who has struggled to eradicate couch grass will know, the more a perennial grass is cut or grazed, the more extensive its spread, because damage to a single shoot will often stimulate dormant buds further down the rhizome to spring into life and, like the sorcerer's apprentice, one problem rapidly divides into many more. In a meadow, this is an advantage, ensuring a dense ground cover of vegetation. Conversely, this cover becomes patchy and dispersed once cutting or grazing ceases, the plants then mutiplying at a more sedate pace.

Some of the best meadow grasses, responding quickly after cutting and producing masses of nutritious foliage, are relatively unattractive for garden use, when you consider how many more ornamental species are available for you to choose from. The commonest, for example, both in meadows and lawn grass mixtures, is the humdrum perennial rye-grass (*Elymus perenne*) and its naturalized cousin *E. multiflorum*, the Italian rye-grass. Oddly enough, some other equally well-known perennial grasses, like couch (*Agropyron repens*) and Yorkshire fog (*Holcus lanatus*) are regarded as weeds of meadows and swamps, because they have low food value and tend to swamp the more valuable species.

Clearly, not every grass is suitable for an authentic meadow, and this applies even more when you are creating in a limited space, where every plant needs to earn its keep. Some of the finer lawn species, which occur here and there in old meadows despite their low agricultural value, can be included in seed mixtures

from top to bottom *Poa annua* (annual meadowgrass) and *Festuca peniculata*.

111

for their good ground-covering qualities combined with a reassuring lack of aggression. These incude the various bents, especially common bent or brown top (*Agrostis tenuis*) and creeping bent (*A. stolonifera*), both tufted turf-forming perennials that thrive on most soils. There is a lovely annual relative, the cloud bent or *A nebulosa*, which produces billowing masses.

Fescues (*Festuca* species) are also fine lawn species, some of them qualifying for meadow status because of their palatability and dependable performance for hay-making. Meadow fescue (*F. pratensis*) is one of the best, growing to 1.2m (4ft) in bold tussocks if left uncut. It is a plant for rich moist soils, unlike the smaller sheep's fescue (*F. ovina)*, which thrives on very poor, dry soils, especially at high altitude. Red fescue and chewings fescue (both subspecies of *F. rubra*) are equally drought-tolerant and occur in the best lawn mixtures. Any or all can be included in meadow seed mixes.

Although authentic, none of these is as exciting visually as the quaking grasses, so-called because of their constant trembling in the lightest breeze. Two species are annuals – the lesser quaking-grass (*Briza minor*) and its large cousin (*B. maxima*) both of which have been cultivated for years in gardens and have escaped to become naturalized in the countryside. The best one for border use is the perennial common quaking-grass (*B. media*) blessed with numerous fascinating alternative names like totter grass, cow quakes and doddering dillies. All these species bear distinctive and graceful branching spikes of pendent locket-shaped flowers, made up of overlapping scales rather like miniature ammonites.

At first sight the quaking grasses look almost too ornamental to be a common wild flower, and yet cow quakes is widespread on chalky soils in Europe and Asia. It deserves a star role in the meadow garden, together with some of the other exotic species that are usually better behaved than most native grasses. One of the largest of these is *Stipa gigantea*, the giant feathergrass. Its name tells you everything, for it can grow to 2.2–2.4m (7–8ft) tall and produces golden stems of open feathery flowers, rather like oats, which stay attractive for weeks, making an irresistible display backlit by the orange glow of an autumn sunset.

Like most feather grasses it is a bulky plant that needs plenty of space, and is best used singly to provide accents in the border, especially if combined with perennials such as fennel and eryngium. Its evergreen clumps of greyish-green leaves reach 90cm (3ft) or more across, making a handsome specimen feature even in winter. Smaller relatives include *S. arundinacea* or pheasant grass, with orange or red striped leaves, *S. barbata*, and the European feather grass (*S. pennata*) whose plumes stream airily in the wind. None of these should exceed about 75cm (30in) high by 90cm (3ft) wide, so you could group a few together to make a really arresting feature.

For a winner at the front of a border, you could hardly better some of the molinias, a very small genus of tufted perennial grasses with neat clumps of foliage and tall upright stems of delicate flowers. There is one British native, the purple moor-grass (*M. caerulea*) a very variable species occurring mainly on damp acid soils and the parent of several good garden forms, bearing flower stems that can be yellow, purple or almost black. All can cope with most kinds of garden soil and are well-behaved, tucking in comfortably among other plants, and their habit is so slender and diaphanous that you can easily glimpse the plants beyond through the most established clump. In its best varieties, such as 'Fontäne' and 'Strahlenquelle' (which means 'gleaming spring' or 'cascade'), the stems form a perfect fountain or vase of elegant seed-heads.

With that kind of distinctive appearance it should be called fountain grass, but that name has already been claimed by another species with arching stems, *Pennisetum alopecuroides*, also known as swamp foxtail grass even though it grows happily in any ordinary well-drained soil. From late summer onwards the dense dome-shaped clumps of flattened deep green leaves are topped by panicles of bristly yellowish or purple flower-heads rather like bottle-brushes, all held well clear of the foliage. It is not reliably hardy in very cold winters without protection, although the variety 'Cassian's Choice' is tougher than most others.

The feather top (*P. villosum*) has a looser habit and white flower spikes that turn purple as they mature, while *P. orientale* is the most appealing of all, with violet-pink flowers and a long flowering season from June onwards. Ranging in height between 45cm and 90cm (18in–3ft), they are all compact and suitable for grouping in borders, although their foliage is not very noteworthy and they need more interesting companions earlier in the year.

In a prairie context, *Elymus* or wild rye grasses are authentic, but choose them cautiously because they are closely related to couch or twitch grass. One of the most dramatic is *Elymus canadensis*, the Canadian wild rye, which spreads (but not invasively) from rhizomatous roots and makes an excellent pioneer species and nurse for other seedling plants. Up to 1.8m (6ft) tall, it has attractive blue-green foliage and nodding heads of red-bristled flowers. The leaves of hairy couch (*E. hispidus*) are an intense blue, and at 75cm (30in) high and only 30cm (12in) across, it is an appealing feature grass for mid-border positions.

Perhaps the most typical prairie grass of them all is *Andropogon gerardii*, the justly named big bluestem that occurs throughout North America, often stretching far to the horizon. Its dense clumps of arching blue-green leaves smoulder in autumn with rich reddish-brown and purple tints, and at 1.5–1.8m (5–6ft) high, a group of these plants would radiate warmth throughout the late meadow garden. They colour best in very poor ground, which also stops them from

cuttings

▨ **Ripe seed-heads of grass feature in the old children's rhyme:**

Tree in summer	(show the seeds)
Tree in winter	(strip seeds with a sweep of the hand)
Bunch of flowers	(show seeds clustered in hand)
April showers	(throw seeds in air).

▨ **Grasses tend to spread far and fast because they have an efficient seeding mechanism. The lightest breeze will fertilize their flowers, and the seeds are a staple food for finches and other birds, which can carry them great distances.**

▨ **In the days of horse-cultivation, the early months of the year were a lean time, when hay replaced the still-dormant grass. Meadow flowers were an important, sometimes medicinal ingredient, and animals often refused hay containing a poor selection of flowers.**

from top to bottom *Stipa gigantea* (giant feathergrass), *Pennisetum villosum* (feather top) and *Andropogon gerardii* (big bluestem).

flopping around loosely, a danger that can lurk in garden soils where the living is too good. If you do not have space for this majestic giant, try the little bluestem, formerly an andropogon, but now renamed *Schizachyrium scoparium*. Only 90cm (3ft) tall, it has all the virtues and flamboyance of its larger cousin, together with whispy plumes of silvery 15cm (6in) flowers that blend perfectly with late flowers such as Michaelmas daisies and rudbeckias.

the annuals

For many years annual flowers received a bad press and were generally disparaged for a number of reasons. In the modern garden their flowering season tended to be rather short and the plants usually needed deadheading to prolong their display. They have a bad habit of self-seeding lavishly, a characteristic that is ideal for natural gardens, but not in tidy designed landscapes. For sophisticated gardeners they often resembled wild flowers too closely and, I suspect, were considered too easy to grow.

Hardy annuals are now coming back into favour as trendy dependable plants. They are, in truth, simple to grow – all you need do is sow them where they are to flower, thin the seedlings if they are overcrowded, and then leave them to perform, which they will do with very little encouragement. And they certainly know how to put on a show. They have only one season in which to produce foliage and flowers, and then to set seed so their offspring can do it all over again, so they do not hang about. To make sure of fertilization amid competition from all around, they tend to have bright or otherwise eye-catching flowers, so you can rely on them for masses of colour, often much more than you would get from a perennial plant.

The trouble is that, although hundreds of annuals grow in the wild, very few are found in established meadows. The dense intertwined ground cover of grasses and perennials ensures that bare places suitable for seedbeds are seldom available, and this can discourage most annual species except right at the start, on bare ground in the process of being colonized. Annual wild flowers tend to be fast-growing pioneers that survive mainly wherever the soil is cultivated, especially in arable fields where a whole flora of endangered cornfield species used to exist. You can explore this range for annuals to sow in a new meadow garden with the first grasses.

Before I look at those though, I want to introduce an annual that certainly does thrive in the oldest meadows, but like them, is threatened by changing practices. Yellow rattle (*Rhinanthus minor*) is an extremely pretty plant with leafy mid-summer spikes of hooded yellow blooms, followed by inflated capsules

that loudly rattle with seeds when disturbed. It grows on most soils, but needs time to settle down in any quantity because it is semi-parasitic on established grasses and lives in cosy intimacy with them. Because of this characteristic it manages to germinate in conditions that would defeat other opportunistic annulas, and it has become of typical of old meadows (and, for obvious reasons, just as endangered). It is one of the first species that you should sow, in autumn with your grass seeds, to establish a truly natural meadow garden.

Cornfield annuals are the ones to choose when starting a meadow on clear cultivated ground, and will give you a lavish display just weeks after sowing – the nearest you can get to instant gardening. They often seed themselves, producing offspring that will flower in their turn during the following few seasons until the grasses and perennials have completely crowded them out. Even then, you could continue to make space for sowing some of your favourites, a method that can be used too in existing rough grass meadows. Alternatively, sow them thinly in seed trays, and when they are large enough, dig out a turf of grass and replace it with the complete trayful of seedlings.

You can buy ready-mixed collections of cornfield annuals and these will vary in their composition, but all are likely to contain poppies of one kind or another. These are some of the most colourful of all annuals, but only survive where the soil is freshly disturbed each year and cannot compete with grasses. Perhaps best known of them all is the common field poppy (*Papaver rhoeas*) with big silky scarlet petals that provide the vitality in the tapestry of traditional cornfield colour. They need to be sown in autumn so that the seeds are exposed to a period of cold weather. Various cultivated selections have added other colours, but none has the same impact as the simple vivid species. It often grows in association with the cornflower (*Centaurea cyanus*) another endangered species in the wild because, as the poet John Clare put it, 'They trouble the cornfields with disturbing beauty'. The single, occasionally double, flowers are generally dark violet-blue, hence the regional name bluebottles, but pink and white forms occur naturally. They are slender plants that benfit from some support, but sow them thickly with other annuals and they should be less inclined to flop about.

Corncockle (*Agrostemma githago*) is very rare in the wild and was driven from arable fields long ago because its poisonous seeds contaminated corn harvests. Its 90cm (3ft) tall flower stems, rising from a thicket of slender blue-green foliage and bearing clear magenta blooms 5cm (2in) across are unmistakable, even if now just a countryside memory for many people, and look spectacular grown en masse or combined when sown in autumn or spring with a pinch of barley or oat seeds for a touch of realism.

Finally corn marigold (*Chrysanthemum segetum*), that other typical member of the arable flora, is slightly shorter than the others that we have looked at, at 50cm (20in). It makes up for lack of height by branching into a satisfying bush of fleshy greyish foliage that continues to produce brash 5cm (2in) golden yellow daisies all summer. Few cultivated annuals can compete with it for sheer brilliance when massed in bold drifts, but for all its beauty it is only locally common now in the wild after centuries of persecution by farmers and even governments – in some countries it was banished by law! It seeds itself lavishly and grows very readily wherever the soil is disturbed, and should continue to dazzle you until the meadow perennials are well established.

The pot marigold (*Calendula officinalis*) is a cultivated cottage garden plant that occasionally escapes onto rough bare ground, and is one of the easiest garden annuals you can choose for a new meadow site. It self-seeds like a wild flower and will pop up year after year at the edge of paths and between paving stones. In the meadow the seeds need bare ground or you can transplant seedlings to thin areas of vegetation, where these sturdy plants will have a head start over competitors, matching them for brilliance and attracting many flying insect species. The typical colour is deep orange-yellow, but varieties exist in a kaleidoscope of red, gold, apricot, cream and even brown shades.

For a real show stopper in the most vivid oranges, reds and yellows, the California poppy (*Eschscholzia californica*) is hard to beat, and you never quite know what colour a bloom will be until it unfurls its paper-thin silky petals over a small 23cm (9in) mound of fine foliage. In its native region of western North America it is actually a short-lived perennial (as well as being the official floral emblem of California), but it is best treated as an annual for sowing directly in spring in poor well-drained soil. You can deadhead plants for continuous flowering, but in a natural context you might prefer to let the long curving seed-pods develop and scatter their contents. The plants will then flower mainly in spring, followed by smaller flushes later in summer and autumn.

from top to bottom *Primula veris* (cowslip), *Eschscholzia californica* (Californian poppy) and *Cerinthe major* 'Purpurascens' (honeywort).

Currently very popular as a fashionable summer annual and wildlife plant to attract nectar-loving insects to the garden, honeywort (*Cerinthe major*) is a southern European species with rather succulent heart-shaped foliage, often spotted with white, and long pendent golden-yellow blooms with a deep red base. The variety 'Purpurascens' is distinguished by its deep purple bracts. Both grow about 60cm (2ft) high and form branching plants with arching stems, so they are often regarded as hanging-basket plants but look fantastic grown at ground level combined with bright yellow flowers such as those of *Eschscholzia californica*, an unusual California poppy.

Some of the fastest-growing flowers are the annual tickseeds, species of coreopsis, many of which are native to North American prairies where they widely colonize drier well-drained soils (there are also fine perennial forms from the same habitats). Among the best of the annuals is the plains coreopsis, *C. tinctoria*, which can race in a few weeks from sowing to a 60–90cm (2–3ft) tangle of slender upright stems, each bearing a solitary 5cm (2in) bright yellow daisy punctuated with a blood-red centre. There are crimson, purple and mahogany varieties, but most of them are much shorter and have none of the impact produced by this wild-looking species.

Add to these some of the other popular cottage garden annuals like white corn-chamomile (*Anthemis arvensis*), love-in-a-mist (*Nigella*), sweet sultan (*Amberboa moschata*) with its fringed heads of white, yellow and pink, and even sunflowers (*Helianthus*) as long as you choose shorter single varieties and avoid the sophisticated doubles. Sow them with cheerful abandon in your new patch, together with a selection of grasses, and even though the border might not look at first quite like a typical natural meadow, it will be a riot of classic cornfield colour that could be repeated in future years in varying degrees of intensity, depending on the growth of the perennials and which annuals manage to find niches still vacant.

the perennials

Moving on to the perennial flowers is like going from poverty to plenty. The permanent nature of a meadow encourages species that can settle in and hang on to their patch from one year to the next, and many perennials take advantage of this relative stability. Their names sound like a roll call from distant summer afternoons in the countryside, which only serves to emphasize their current predicament as habitats dwindle and numbers decline.

There was a time, for example, when you could find cowslips (*Primula veris*) in meadows everywhere in such abundance that the flowers were gathered by

the armful for May Day and Cowslip Sunday festivals. With the loss of so many permanent meadows, they are now more likely to be found speckling waysides and road verges where modern mowing regimes suit their growth cycle and they are relatively safe from disturbance. They are an essential ingredient of the natural hay meadow, where they seem happiest among the rough grass that is not grazed or mown until they have set their mid-summer seeds.

Another species that has dwindled in recent years in meadows (although still widespread on sandy dunes and elsewhere) is the common bird's-foot trefoil (*Lotus corniculatus*), just one of several pea-like plants with yellow flowers, but by far the prettiest and an important food plant for bees and blue butterflies. A variable species with 40cm (16in) stems that usually sprawl in a low carpet of foliage, it is a motley mixture of colours in full bloom: its buds are deep red, almost crimson, and unfurl into clusters of clear, bright yellow pea-flowers tinted here and there with orange, light red or brown. Sow it outdoors in the autumn and let winter break down the tough seedcoat, or rub the seeds between two sandpaper blocks before sowing in spring.

A close relative is common restharrow (*Ononis repens*), a pink-flowered pea that is really a shrub, not that you would notice. Spreading or creeping to about 60cm (2ft), it has slightly fibrous stems and even woodier roots that often got tangled round ploughs and other cultivating tools, halting their progress – hence restharrow. It is a native of grasslands, but only on the lightest soils, where it often mixes with bird's-foot trefoil and lady's bedstraw (*Galium verum*), one of many bedstraws that colonize various kinds of habitat, but the only one with golden yellow flowers (others are white). The tiny fragrant blooms are packed in dense clusters at the tops of upright 75–80cm (30–32in) stems, and it spreads amiably through grassland with underground runners.

Lady's bedstraw flowers in July and August, about the same time as small scabious (*Scabiosa columbaria*) – the two together would make an outstanding combination on light or chalky soils. Its bluish-violet flowers that never seem to stop all summer are pale and dainty, suggesting a weak plant, but it is in fact sturdy enough to support its 75cm (30in) stems without flopping, and cheerfully jostles for space with other summer-flowering meadow perennials such as the large white-flowered oxeye daisy (*Leucanthemum vulgare*), which can fill a new meadow with bloom until the competition is established. Soft pink common valerian (*Valeriana officinalis*) is another suitable candidate for a pioneer mixture, whether your ground is light or heavy, moist or dry.

Finally, no meadow flora would be complete without a buttercup. I'm not talking about the invasive creeping buttercup whose long, tough runners studded with new plants you probably spend hours forking out of herbaceous borders, but a much more appealing species, the bulbous buttercup (*Ranunculus bulbosus*). This gets its name from the swollen underground stem-base, which produces rosettes of prettily lobed leaves that often die down right out of sight for a while in midsummer, at the end of its long display of large bright yellow blooms that start appearing as early as March. It is a charming species, much less villainous than some buttercups, and grows widely in dryish grassland, especially on chalk.

Among the garden plants you could introduce is another buttercup, *Ranunculus acris* 'Flore Pleno', the double form of the meadow buttercup with all that species' dazzling good looks but thankfully free from its vices. This looks like a buttercup on steroids, with exuberant masses of egg-yolk-yellow double blooms in perfect rosettes on wiry 90cm (3ft) stalks.

If all this vivid yellow is too garish for you, cool the scheme down a little by adding some blue flowers, starting with *Scabiosa caucasica*, the familiar perennial scabious of borders and florists' shops, which starts blooming in June and often continues into autumn. The plain species has wide pale or lavender-blue flowers as much as 8cm (3in) across, but you can dial up virtually any blue shade you can think of, together with several good white varieties. Despite their long season the flowers often exhaust themselves in early autumn, which is when *Verbena bonariensis* really gets into its stride. In borders this lilac-blue perennial can often look out of place, especially where single plants are dotted here and there. It grows 1.5–1.8m (5–6ft) or more, and can tower rather ridiculously over its neighbours unless several plants are grouped together as a more substantial feature or are partnered by companions of similar height.

One of these could be Joe Pye weed (*Eupatorium purpureum*), a plant that somehow epitomises the prairie garden in most people's minds. It is a majestic giant, growing up to 2.4m (8ft) tall and 1.2m (4ft) wide, and prefers moister soils, rather like its British relative hemp-agrimony (*E. cannabinum*) which could be grown with it as a paler companion, especially in its soft rose double form 'Flore Pleno'. Although the purplish blooms of Joe Pye weed share the same part of the colour spectrum as the verbena, the flower shape is sufficiently different for them to maintain their distinctiveness. Combine with that other tall stalwart, *Vernonia crinita* or ironweed, add a sprinkle of yellow with *Silphium laciniatum*, the compass plant, and you have a realistic prairie garden.

So far I have not mentioned campanulas, often the first name that springs to mind at the mention of blue flowers. There is a bellflower for every situation, and one of the most statuesque is *Campanula lactiflora*; 'Prichards Variety' has vibrant lavender-blue flowers on strong stems that easily reach 1.5m (5ft), raising the display to eye-level. It grows almost anywhere, even in very rough grass, unlike the essential campanula of short thin grass, the harebell (*C. rotundifolia*).

cuttings

■ With its cheerful and innocent blooms, blue scabious is one of the prettiest meadow flowers but its name recalls a less charming historical connection, for it was once used to treat plague and scabies or 'scab'. Perhaps its local name, gypsy rose, might be preferable.

■ Bird's-foot trefoil occurs almost everywhere and has collected over 70 regional names, including grannies' toenails, eggs and bacon, cuckoo's stockings and Dutchman's clogs, most of them referring to the long and distinctive claw-like seed-pods.

■ Lady's bedstraw got its name from its use to stuff mattresses, particularly those of women about to give birth. It must have been a pleasant species to use, because when dried it has a strong scent of newly mown hay.

■ The annual common vetch or tare was a popular agricultural forage crop, but its perennial cousins were ancient pests. A biblical parable refers to them being gathered first for burning, before the good wheat was harvested and stored.

from top to bottom *Verbena bonariensis* (Argentinian verbain), *Eupatorium purpureum* (Joe Pye weed) and *Campanula lactiflora* (milky bellflower).

plants for a meadow garden

grasses

Miscanthus sinensis
'Silberfeder' (syn. 'Silver Feather') eulalia grass
height 2.4m (8ft).
spread 90cm–1.2m (3–4ft).
habit Hardy deciduous perennial grass.
season Foliage summer–autumn; flowers September–winter.
site Full sun, in any moist well-drained soil.
characteristics A dense and steadily expanding clump of tough narrow leaves, upright then arching outwards from mid-height. Abundant tall panicles of feathery pinkish-brown flowers, which turn silver as they mature. Dislikes wet soil.
how to grow Plant in spring and feed with general fertilizer during the early slow development. Cut off dead flowers and leaves in spring or surface tidy (birds often nest in the thicket of dead leaves).
note Excellent prairie plant; good with Joe Pye weed, echinacea and cosmos.

Stipa tenuissima
(syn. S. tenuifolia) feather grass
height 60cm (2ft).
spread 60cm (2ft).
habit Hardy deciduous or semi-evergreen perennial grass.
season Foliage spring–autumn; flowers May–July.
site Full sun, in medium or light well-drained soil.
characteristics Very upright tufted clumps of densely packed pale yellow-green leaves, very fine and sometimes tightly rolled, topped in summer by silky, rippling or softly nodding masses of slim feathery greenish-buff flowers that last for many weeks.
how to grow Plant in spring and keep well-watered in dry weather while young. Leave foliage over winter, and tidy or cut right down in spring.
note Plant in groups for maximum impact. S. tirsa is half this size and a better choice for small borders.

annuals

Borago officinalis
borage
height 60cm (2ft).
spread 45cm (18in).
habit Hardy annual.
season Flowers summer.
site Full sun or very light shade, on any well-drained soil.
characteristics A stout but often sprawling clump of hairy main stems, with greyish green leaves and branching heads of semi-pendent star-shaped flowers, usually bright rich blue, but occasionally white (f. alba). Continues flowering prolifically all summer, and attracts large numbers of bees.
how to grow Sow in spring or autumn where plants are to grow. Plants self-seed liberally and can even become invasive, but seedlings are easily thinned or transplanted.
note The leaves have a cucumber flavour, while the flowers look great floating in summer drinks. Sow as a pioneer annual and harvest freely.

Consolida ajacis
(syn. C. ambigua) larkspur
height 30–90cm (12in–3ft).
spread 23–30cm (9–12in).
habit Hardy annual.
season Flowers spring or summer.
site Full sun, in fertile slightly alkaline soils.
characteristics Slender plants like miniature delphiniums, varying in size according to variety. Fine ferny leaves and branching spikes of single or double flowers in shades of pink, white or blue, but poisonous seeds.
how to grow Sow where plants are to grow, in autumn for spring flowering or spring for summer displays. Support taller kinds with sticks or neighbours. Deadhead to prolong flowering or leave to set seed.
note Although a familiar garden flower, the wild species comes from Asian and European steppes.

Vicia sativa
common vetch, annual tare
height Up to 90cm (3ft).
spread 10–15cm (4–6in).
habit Hardy annual.
season Flowers May–September.
site Full sun, in any fairly fertile soil.
characteristics A versatile climbing or trailing annual, shorter in bare soil but scrambling with tendrils on host plants to flower in the sun. Slim rich green leaves, with up to 8 pairs of small leaflets, and mauve or purplish-red flowers in pairs at the base of each, followed by long hairy seed-pods. Self-seeds freely.
how to grow Often added to meadow seed mixtures. Surface sow in spring and tread into the soil.
note If possible, grow subsp. nigra, which is the true wild form, whereas subsp. sativa is a coarser agricultural selection.

Aster cordifolius
'Silver Spray'
height 1.2m (4ft).
spread 45–60cm (18in–2ft).
habit Hardy herbaceous perennial.
season Flowers August–October.
site Full sun or light shade, in moist fertile soils.
characteristics A particularly choice variety, making strong clumps of tall sturdy stems with feathery mid-green leaves and large loose heads of pale lilac-pink 4cm (1½in) daisies infused with an overall silvery-white glow.
how to grow Plant and mulch annually in spring. Divide every few years in spring or autumn as clumps become weak or diffuse.
note The blue wood aster, from which this is derived, enjoys the shaded edges of meadows. For really hot sunny spots, try the many varieties of A. amellus, the Italian aster.

Miscanthus sinensis 'Silberfeder' (eulalia grass)

Stipa tenuissima (feather grass)

Borago officinalis (borage)

Vicia sativa (common vetch)

Catananche caerulea

cupid's dart

height 60–90cm (2–3ft).

spread 30cm (12in).

habit Hardy herbaceous short-lived perennial.

season Flowers July–September.

site Full sun, in any well-drained soil.

characteristics A loose basal clump of narrow grassy leaves, radiating like a dandelion from a strong crown, and slender bare stems crowned with solitary 5cm (2in) lilac-blue flowers with distinctive bracts.

how to grow Plant in spring. Divide or take root cuttings every 2–3 years to keep plants vigorous. Alternatively sow in spring or autumn as a hardy annual or biennial.

note A dry meadow plant from southern Europe, happy among grasses but only long-lived in hot well-drained places. 'Major' is a popular but untidy lavender-blue form.

Eucomis pallidiflora

giant pineapple flower

height 60–75cm (24–30in).

spread 60cm (2ft).

habit Slightly tender bulbous perennial.

season Flowers August–September.

site Full sun, in well-drained soil that is fairly dry in winter.

characteristics A robust basal rosette of strap-shaped, glossy light green leaves with crinkled edges that arch up to 75cm (30in) long. Sturdy spikes are packed with greenish-white star-shaped flowers, topped with a tuft of small leaves and followed by conspicuous purplish-maroon seed capsules.

how to grow Plant bulbs 15cm (6in) deep in spring. Mulch in autumn or dig up and overwinter indoors in pots. Divide clumps when they become congested.

note Although hardier than other eucomis species, it is best lifted annually where winters are cold and wet.

Penstemon 'White Bedder'

height 60cm (24in).

spread 45cm (18in).

habit Fairly hardy herbaceous or semi-evergreen perennial.

season Flowers July–September.

site Full sun, in any well-drained soil.

characteristics A handsome free-flowering penstemon cultivar, producing compact bushes of erect stems with relatively large narrow leaves, and strong upright spikes of large white blooms with a creamy tinge, emerging from pink buds and turning pink-tinted with maturity.

how to grow Plant in spring. Cut back fairly hard after flowering to conserve energy. In cold areas take late cuttings as insurance, and mulch plants with tree leaves.

note For authenticity, look out for endangered P. grandiflorus, the large beard-tongue with masses of lavender-blue flowers marked with magenta.

Rudbeckia 'Goldquelle'

coneflower

height 90cm (3ft).

spread 60–90cm (2–3ft).

habit Hardy herbaceous rhizomatous perennial.

season Flowers July–October.

site Full sun, in loamy well-drained soil.

characteristics Compact, fairly loose clumps of tall wiry stems, each with a few large divided leaves at the base, getting smaller further up towards the heads of double dahlia-like flowers, bright lemon-yellow with greenish centres and slightly drooping petals.

how to grow Plant and mulch annually in spring. Pull or fork up creeping underground stems if these become intrusive.

note Derived from single-flowered R. laciniata, the cut-leaved coneflower from North America that grows 1.8m (6ft) tall and looks great as a prairie plant.

Salvia x sylvestris 'Mainacht' (syn. 'May Night')

height 75cm (30in).

spread 45cm (18in).

habit Hardy herbaceous perennial.

season Foliage spring–autumn; flowers May–July.

site Full sun, in light well-drained soil.

characteristics A strong bushy plant forming a solid clump of branching stems bearing hairy and wrinkled, heart-shaped mid-green leaves and masses of long dense spires of large indigo-blue flowers with a hint of purple-black.

how to grow Plant in spring and water occasionally during dry weather in the first year. Protect dormant plants with a mulch of tree leaves in cold areas.

note One of the parents of this dependable hybrid is S. pratensis, the native meadow clary, which revels in dryish grassland.

Verbascum chaixii

nettle-leaved mullein

height 90cm (3ft).

spread 45cm (18in).

habit Hardy semi-evergreen perennial.

season Flowers June–August.

site Full sun, in poor, slightly alkaline well-drained soils.

characteristics Clumps of large basal rosettes of hairy greyish-green leaves that are long, scalloped and sometimes lobed. Stout white-felted stems bear small leaves and are wreathed in soft yellow flowers with purple eyes.

how to grow Plant in autumn or spring, in poor soil to avoid soft vigorous growth that might need support. May also be grown from seeds sown in a seed-bed in late spring or early summer.

note The white form 'Album' of this eye-catching Mediterranean species is even finer, with clear mauve-pink eyes and naturalizing well in prairie schemes.

Catananche caerulea (cupid's dart)

Eucomis pallidiflora (giant pineapple flower)

Rudbeckia 'Goldquelle' (coneflower)

a season

in the natural meadow garden

It ought to be clear by now that the special character of a meadow garden is entirely due to the way it is managed, so you should abandon any illusions that you just sow it and leave it for nature to do the rest! On the other hand, the work that does need doing is very infrequent and straightforward, complicated only by any differences in the type of meadow – whether it is a spring-flowering lawn, a summer water meadow or a dry prairie, for example. The most effort you have to put in is probably concentrated in the initial planning, preparation and planting. You can use a piecemeal approach when converting an existing lawn or paddock into a wild flower meadow, introducing groups of pot-grown plants or sowing the odd bare patch wherever the fancy takes you. Laying out a complete border is more like painting with plants, and you will probably find it much easier to achieve the effect you want if you empty the ground of all existing plants, including perennial weeds you might prefer not to include in the final collection. Rake the surface level and then broadcast a seed mixture over the whole area for an unplanned mix of plants. Alternatively, use a stick or bottleful of dry sand to draw the outline of patches on the surface, and sow different species in these areas.

If you are using young plants, arrange them all on the surface before putting them in. Make sure you have several of each kind, position the first as a centre plant and then group the others informally to make it look as if the central one has set seed all around, even placing one or two some distance away among neighbouring groups for a really naturalistic look. Let the different kinds infiltrate and blend into each other, and don't feel obliged to put larger plants at the back of the border, with small ones at the front; looking through the waving stems of a tall grass to a smaller plant behind is all part of the scheme. Try to use roughly equal numbers of each species, and plant as close as you dare – nature rarely leaves gaps and any bare ground might be colonized by weeds, while crowding the plants will remove the need for staking taller kinds.

spring

planting – Most of this planting can be done in the spring, when the weather is more inviting and the plants are ready to start growing, but you will probably need to water occasionally during the summer while they become established. You might prefer to plant in autumn, especially with early-flowering species that can settle in before the colder months arrive and then concentrate all their energy on flowering in the spring.

sowing – Prepare seed-beds now by forking and raking the surface to a fine tilth. If you are choosing the cornfield wild flower option, broadcast a mixture of annuals over the surface: to ensure a thorough coverage, walk up and down the patch scattering half the seeds thinly but evenly, and then do it again at right angles, sowing the other half across the plot. Then lightly rake the seeds in or simply tread over the whole area to press them into contact with the soil. Before sowing you can add an equal amount of cereal seeds, preferably barley or oats, to the mixture for a really authentic look. You should not have to re-sow the following spring, but you might need to till the surface with a rake or pronged hoe to disturb the seeds that have been scattered naturally and ensure an equally impressive display.

You can use the same mixture even when sowing a perennial meadow, because the annuals will give you a good show the same year while the perennials and grasses establish themselves quietly beneath. If you look at any cornfield when the crop has been cleared, you will see a green carpet of plants through the stubble, and these would soon turn the arable field into a meadow if they were not ploughed in after harvest. Alternatively use a really good meadow seed mix that contains about 80% grasses and the rest a blend of annual and perennial seeds to suit your soil type, and sow this in the same way.

weeding – During the early years and even later, when the meadow is established, you will find unwelcome visitors trying to muscle in. Thistle, nettle, dock and willowherb seeds will find their way to your patch by various means, and you need to check every month or two that they have not sneaked in unobserved and started to take over. Remove them while they are still small and you will not disturb everything else growing in their vicinity. Pull them up by hand or carefully fork them out. Spot-treatment with a systemic herbicide is another option, or you can follow custom by burning them. This was part of traditional management routines in prairies, where vast stretches were set alight every few years to control more vigorous species and gently fertilize plants with the resulting potash. This is not something to imitate on a large scale in the garden, especially later when top growth is dry and inflammable, but destroying weeds

cuttings

■ Cultivated perennials often run out of steam after a few years and need to be divided in autumn or early spring. Dig up the entire plant with as much root as possible, and chop it into portions with a spade. Throw away any geriatric parts, re-plant the younger sections and give away the leftovers.

■ Plants in a prairie scheme should be strong enough to hold each other up, but if they need a little help you can use 'pea sticks', branches of deciduous trees and shrubs pushed into the ground so their twiggy growth provides unobtrusive support for the perennials.

■ Removing the flowering stems of most perennials soon after the first flowers fade can often stimulate a second set of blooms. Leave these alone when they finish, because they supply seeds for birds (and for you!) and also homes for overwintering beneficial insects like the aphid-eating lacewing.

with a flame gun is an established non-chemical method and could be used to advantage where there is no risk of fire spreading.

Spring is a good time to start looking for weeds, because you will also find seedlings from your own plants starting to appear everywhere, sometimes where you would rather not have them, but often in more imaginative spots than your original scheme allowed for. This is the way a natural meadow changes gradually and unpredictably from year to year. There will usually be too many of these self-setters, for nature is unbelievably prodigal, but you can thin over-crowded colonies, transplant seedlings elsewhere if you have a better idea, or just leave them to fight it out.

feeding – Opinions vary on the subject of feeding wild flowers. On the one hand, traditional grazing patterns for at least part of the year meant that the flowers and grasses were manured, but it is also true that fertilizers can stimulate rank growth, encouraging the more vigorous species at the expense of the weaker (sometimes more desirable) plants. A practical compromise would be to adjust feeding to fine-tune local or individual growth rates, using it to boost ailing plants or your personal favourites for example, while withholding extra nutrients from the others. Make sure first that your target plants do not actually prefer impoverished soil – a well-fed mullein, for example, will flop all over the place – and only use organic materials such as garden compost or small amounts of well-rotted manure. Chemical fertilizers are far too concentrated and quite unsuitable for this delicate kind of eco-system.

mowing – A wild flower lawn or small back garden meadow needs a mowing routine to keep plants thriving as they would in the countryside. If you are growing spring-flowering species, either abandon all mowing until mid-summer or give the area a single cut in March, using a rotary mower set at it its highest – at least 5cm (2in) and preferably as high as 10cm (4in). This will simply top all the growth, evening up the appearance and then leaving the plants to grow on and flower at the appropriate time. You do not need to mow again until they have seeded in July, after which you can cut it at regular intervals as if it were being grazed after hay-harvest. Alternatively, just mow or scythe once in July and leave to grow again for a possible autumn flush of flowers.

After mowing, leave the clippings lying on the ground for a few days for all the seeds to fall out, and then rake them up or mow again, this time with the grass-box in place to catch the clippings. Another way, used by some local authorities to gradually extend wild-flower areas, is to collect the mowings first time round and spread them on a fresh patch of prepared ground where they will act as a short-term mulch while the seeds they contain fall through and germinate to create a new stretch of wild flower meadow or lawn.

summer

mowing – Mid-summer marks the critical time for mowing meadows, when you can either cut down the seeded flowers and grasses in a spring scheme, or stop mowing where a late summer and autumn display is preferred. Very tall growth might defeat the most robust rotary or scythe mower, in which case you will need to learn how to use a sickle or hand-held scythe. These are not as difficult to handle as you might think, but they can be dangerous, especially if you stand with your feet in the wrong place! Practise cautiously until you get into a rhythm, and keep the cutting edge very sharp by honing it with a sharpening stone at frequent intervals – the old scythes-men used to pause every time they reached the side of the field, partly to stretch their backs but mainly to touch up the edge of the blade.

If you use a sickle or 'grass-hook', make yourself a 'hooting stick' from a straight length of branch with the stump of a side shoot at the far end – use this in your other hand to pull the top growth away as you cut, and you will find the

Don't be too eager to weed the meadow in spring. Many grasses and flowering species, such as these fritillaries, will self seed to create natural drifts.

The essence of any meadow scheme is to produce a wild, natural-looking feature – and that includes fauna as well as flora.

other work much easier as well as safer: never, ever use your free hand instead, and keep it well away from the blade at all times.

autumn

sowing and planting – You can sow and plant new perennials and many annuals in autumn instead of spring, and this can be preferable where the ground is still moist and warm, but not on heavier ground that might lie cold and wet all winter. It is a particularly good time for planting existing lawns, after the main mowing season comes to an end and the grass growth is slowing down. Cut the turf short and plant individual pot-grown perennials in natural drifts, using a trowel or bulb-planter to make the holes, or cut out turf with a spade, arrange several plants in each patch and then scatter some annual seeds in the spaces in between. Early autumn is also the season for planting bulbs, and there are many species that colonize damper meadows once these are established. The bulbs of the wild daffodil (*Narcissus pseudonarcissus*), snake's-head fritillery (*Fritillaria meleagris*) and the yellow wild tulip (*Tulipa sylvestris*) can all be planted 10–15cm (4–6in) deep in random groups, or you can raise them from seed added to your sowing mixture. Some nurseries sell tubers of the common spotted orchid, (*Dactylorhiza fuchsii*), which is surprisingly easy to grow in alkaline grass.

division – The essence of any meadow scheme is to produce a natural-looking feature, resisting the temptation to be a dictator and organize plants in rows and ranks – that is traditional kitchen gardening practice and has no value in the wild. Instead, allow plants to spread where they will by runners or seeds, and let serendipity have a hand in your grand design. Some plants are bound to become over-enthusiastic and threaten to swamp their neighbours, and the way to deal with this is to divide the offending plant now or in the spring and re-plant in soil that you have refreshed with compost. Sooner or later you will probably have to do this with many perennials that decline with age.

winter

To appreciate the spectacular effect of an early morning frost on gently waving seed-heads, you have to resist any temptation to be tidy. Prairie meadow borders in particular have an extremely long flowering season, with the rudbeckias, asters and other late species often flowering well into October. Once these stalwarts have ceased blooming, ingrained herbaceous border habits might compel you to cut off all the faded top growth ready for the plants' winter sleep.

Resist this urge and leave everything alone over winter. The reason for this is not purely aesthetic, even though the seed-heads of many plants and the yellow and brown shades of their dead foliage are stunningly beautiful. The old stems also form a protective cage above the crown of the plant, helping plants of borderline hardiness – some penstemons, for example – to survive the harshest frosts. If you remove the stems, winter rainfall then has a direct route down the open stem-base and into the heart of the plant, possibly causing rot.

The time to tidy perennials in the prairie is right at the end of winter, when the earth is about to warm up and stimulate the plants to push up fresh green shoots. You can safely remove all the old top growth then, cutting it with shears, a sickle or a strimmer. Gather up the debris and compost it or heap it around the edges of the border as a refuge for small animals. If you are growing greedy plants or growth has not matched your hopes, you could then spread a generous mulch of compost over the border, avoiding the emerging shoots.

In a meadow's early years, this mulch will provide nutrients for the coming season and help to keep the soil moist. Once perennial growth is established, however, there will be little bare ground to mulch and the plants will have become relatively self-sufficient. At that stage you will find that one or two cuts of top growth annually, plus a few checks for weed seedlings is all you need to do. Those first few years of careful tending will have produced a natural feature that could survive for centuries, giving you your very own flowering meadow.

the natural

Woodlands form a lively community of plants – from the trees and their spreading branches, to the woody plants and shrubs below, and down to the low-level herbaceous layer. You can echo this woodland planting in a relatively small space – with just a single tree underplanted with a vibrant mixture of small shrubs and bulbs.

woodland garden

origins

of the natural woodland garden

I find woods are some of the most peaceful places on earth, where any sounds from without are muffled by millions of leaves gently brushing one against the other, and the incessant birdsong and background hum of insects reminds you that this is a very special environment filled with abundant life.

Woods have not always been regarded as calm, refreshing oases where people can wander in search of peace and quiet, and not so many centuries

ago, when there was more forest than now, they were thought to be places of mystery and intrigue, their dark canopies and dense vegetation filled with evil noises and shadows. Tree myths and legends sprang up, from reassuring tales of good spirits like the Green Man personified in the stories of Robin Hood, to murmured accounts of monsters and wild beasts used to scare children.

Even now, when woodlands account for a small fraction of the countryside, it is possible to lose your bearings among the trees, and start to hear whisperings and strange noises once you realize you have been going round in fruitless circles. This must have been much more terrifying when the dense wild wood stretched over much of the country. Just how much of the British Isles was covered in forest in historical times has been the subject of heated debate between botanists and historians for many years, but the general consensus now is that 95–97% of the land was forested when Stone Age hunters and gatherers arrived from the European mainland about 3,500 years ago.

Much earlier there were other forests that came and went. Britain was once a tropical paradise of rainforest, made up of unbelievably huge mosses, ferns and horsetails that later died and decayed to eventually form coal seams. About

Even deep within a forest of trees, shafts of sunlight pierce the scheme.

cuttings

300 million years ago, climate change replaced these with deserts and sand-dunes, which gave way in their turn to a sub-tropical tree cover of more familiar species such as conifers, magnolias and palms. These disappeared when the ice ages clamped down on the country, killing all but a few mosses that lingered on at the edge of the ice sheet.

When this receded about 10,000 years ago, the land was left bare of plant life. But nature never sits still for long, and very quickly colonies of mosses, lichens and small flowering plants began to green up the barren earth at the start of the pleasantly temperate era we know and live in. Once this colonization had started the trees could begin to move in, not the rich and diverse mix that we recognize now as woodland, but hardy pioneer species such as willows, birches and junipers. These were followed from the Continent as conditions improved by hazel, rowan and Scots pine, which was the strongest of them all and took the lead until pine forests covered much of the country.

About 3,000 years later sea levels rose and Britain became separated from the rest of Europe, so that only the more mobile species could spread here naturally – trees like oak, ash, wych-elm and alder. That is why botanists consider there are only 35 different native British trees and all others, such as larches and silver firs, have been deliberately introduced since. As the climate continued to warm up, these now resident species were able to flourish and gradually overwhelmed the pines, slowly producing the kind of rich broad-leaved forest that can still be found in the lowlands, where a mixture of tree types generally dominated by oak is typical. You can still see remnants of the earlier ancient pine forests in the Scottish Highlands, where the harsher climate discouraged oak from venturing very far.

This is the kind of landscape Stone Age settlers found and started to clear to make room for their settlements. From then until the twentieth century the forest cover steadily dwindled. To successive generations the woods were rich, unlimited resources that could be plundered freely. Their edges provided refuge for settlements, clearings could be used for grazing pigs and other livestock, and the trees themselves supplied timber for making charcoal and house-building or ship construction. By the end of the First World War, during which home-grown timber was felled at an alarming rate to replace imports, only about 4% of the British countryside was covered with woodland.

Although we still use vast amounts of timber from managed woodlands and planted forests, the woods that remain are now appreciated for their aesthetic beauty and environmental value to wildlife. We understand their delicate eco-systems better, and planting trees to produce new woods has become a popular activity in an attempt to halt habitat loss for wildlife and to compensate for climate change. Translating woodland into our domestic gardens as a natural landscape feature is one way to balance the destruction of natural tree-cover, but to do this effectively we need to analyze the structure of a typical wood.

It is much more than a simple canopy of tall plants, and in reality is as diverse as any other ecosystem. Many of the plants growing there do so very slowly and you might think a wood looks the same from one year to the next, but steady change, movement and succession are taking place all the time. A thriving woodland contains trees of every age, from freshly germinating seedlings and sprouting whips – young, single-stemmed trees without any branches – on through juvenile plants to tall mature specimens.

The basic structure of any tree develops to produce the largest possible leaf-surface area in the available space, with branches reaching up high to capture all the sunlight they can. The tree that manages to do this first reaps all the light, in the process restricting its competitors' access to the sun by shading and crowding out their growth. Life in the forest is quite simply a race to the top. Although this ruthless competition takes place in slow motion, with many trees needing 150 years or more to reach their full potential, the same pressures that urge weed seedlings to spring from germination to maturity in less than a year also apply to trees growing in forests by their thousand.

The tree that grows tallest and fastest triumphs over slower species, which are then suppressed and can only wait until the death or injury of a dominant tree opens up an opportunity for them to scramble towards the light. Perhaps there is something sinister about life in the forest after all!

the majesty of trees

One of our earliest family photographs shows me riding on my dad's back as he strides in dappled sunlight through a dense forest of conifers. I think this early interaction with trees must have had a profound effect on me, because I went as a toddler straight from growing cress on the window-sill to germinating tree seedlings.

Ever since then I have had an abiding love for woods and trees, the grandest of all plants. Although I find great cathedrals and castles impressive, they are easily surpassed by the emotional response I feel towards majestic trees as soon as I enter a woodland.

It is not just their scale and grandeur. There is personality too, with the fissured bark of many looking just like the lines on an old man's face and giving the trees profound character. Without wishing to sound like a total tree-hugger, to plant a tree is to leave something a bit special for the next generations.

identifying
the potential woodland garden

All this discussion of trees and their behaviour might sound as though growing your own woodland is like gardening on such a grand scale as to be prohibitive for the domestic plot, but this is not so. Whether you have the space for a large copse of robust native trees or just a couple of dainty ornamentals, introducing them into your garden will create a unique environment that is perfect for a whole host of shade-loving plants. It takes more than a few trees to make up a woodland community, and it is these other plants that can help you decide how to translate the natural wood into garden terms.

Botanists and foresters see woodland as a series of layers that interact with each other. As we have just seen, the largest trees form the top or climax layer, the upper canopy with a spreading array of branches and foliage basking in full sun. Below this is a mixed group of largely woody plants – shrubs and smaller

When the canopy of leaves has fallen the resulting higher light levels allow the woodland floor to erupt in bloom.

trees able to tolerate dappled shade, younger climax trees waiting for an opportunity to burst through the top, and scrub plants like blackberries and wild roses. These are grouped together as the shrub layer or understorey. The lowest tier of plants comprises bulbs, grasses and herbaceous wild flowers, and is known quite simply as the ground or herbaceous layer.

You can recreate this lively community in your garden from the top down, by planting trees in a bare piece of ground and establishing other plants beneath as they grow, or the other way round, by imitating the natural succession of plants, from the first herbaceous species to the final climax trees. Much depends on what you already have in the way of a potentially suitable site, starting with the soil type and condition.

An essential preliminary step is to carry out a simple pH test to find out whether your soil is acid or alkaline or, most likely, somewhere in between. The point of this is more to eliminate those plants that would be unhappy there, rather than to identify the ones you should grow. This will only establish the acidity levels of the topsoil, however, and it is possible that your garden might lie on a deep bed of alkaline chalk or acid greensand, so you should confirm this test by noticing the type of trees that grow in nearby woods and hedgerows.

Fertility or the lack of it is not a great problem. Trees only really require good food supplies while young, and most garden soils can supply much more than the typical sites used for successful woodland and forest planting. Some trees specialize in coping with mean conditions, though, and conifers are particularly suitable for impoverished and shallow soils, their many fibrous roots allowing them to extract the most meagre resources from quite unpromising sites. They are also good in other ways when the going gets tough: their reduced leaf-size and the protective waxy layer that coats every needle help them tolerate high winds and adverse weather conditions. Their only Achilles' heel is that many cannot stand wet ground, and prefer well-drained or sloping sites, hence their use commercially on steep hillsides rather than lowland plains.

This is where the broad-leaved deciduous trees fare best, with their probing structural roots perfectly designed for extracting water and nutrients from deep fertile land. They are less likely to succeed in exposed conditions, because their relatively soft flat leaves are easily dried and destroyed by high wind. Deciduous woodlands tend to develop in valleys and lush lowland plains protected by hillsides, whereas conifers have been relegated to the highlands, although they make excellent windbreaks and shelter belts that can be planted around deciduous trees to help them survive and develop healthily.

At an early stage during your plans for a woodland garden, remember that trees do not have very deep roots on the whole, but tend to spread sideways,

much further than you might expect and well beyond the area shaded by their canopy, so you should keep them away from houses, walls and pavements. In a mixed garden you might also find their questing roots dominating nearby areas such as a kitchen garden or pond. Give them plenty of space, though, and you will find that their unique eco-system – cooler in summer and protected in winter, with plenty of lush growth in their dappled shade – will be a continual delight.

You do not need a large area of land to create a woodland planting area, a single silver birch, rowan or weeping ash can cast sufficient shade. Two or three existing large apple trees are enough to create a really effective top storey, allowing you to grow shade-tolerant species underneath and giving you crops of fruit as a bonus. Your nearest trees might be next door or in the street outside, in which case you can 'borrow' them as part of your landscape. And remember that hedges are important corridors of shrubs that will blend into your woodland, and even walls and fences can be planted with wild or culti-vated climbers to become part of the complex mixture of plants.

If you are creating a woodland area from scratch, you need to decide if you want your trees to grow and gain height fast, or whether you are content to plant a whole community and let it develop more naturally but, inevitably, more slowly. Planting trees for rapid growth involves keeping the ground underneath

clear of other vigorous plants for the first few years, at least until the trees are about 1.5–1.8m (5–6ft) high, because competition holds back growth considerably. You could plant a few patches of wild flowers here and there at first, but not the whole range of understorey and ground-level species.

On the other hand you might prefer to adopt a more natural, leisurely approach, planting up the patch first with herbaceous species that thrive in sun or enjoy a little dappled shade. Combine these with a few choice shrubs, interplanting what will look like a mixed border for a few years with a blend of 'nurse' and young climax trees (see page 138). The nurse trees will shoot away rapidly, sheltering the slower climax species and creating the beginnings of a canopy that will gradually discourage some of the sun-loving herbaceous plants. All you do then is replace them in the increasingly dappled light with shade-lovers, and eventually the nurse trees will become redundant and can be removed, leaving you with all the elements of a young woodland.

The results of either method will eventually be the same, although one will give you an instant but gradually changing garden, while the other might look like a tree plantation for the first few years. Which approach you choose depends on whether you prefer dynamic revolution or gentle evolution as a guiding principle for introducing your woodland plants.

137

plants

of the natural woodland garden

As will be clear by now, an established wood is a cosmopolitan mixture of trees and plants, each doing different important jobs in a state of slightly precarious but mutually supportive stability. In a new wood, however, the different growth rates of each plant type are much more obvious, and you need to plan carefully and intervene occasionally to steer and balance their individual development. To help differentiate between the different plant types, I propose looking separately at each group: the trees, which I have divided into two types (nurse trees and climax species), shrubs and scrub, which compose the understorey, and the ground layer of bulbs and herbaceous plants – this is sometimes subdivided into a field layer of plants above 15cm (6in) high and a true ground layer of species shorter than that, but I shall treat them as one in a garden context.

nurse trees

There always has to be a first past the post, and in the case of a developing woodland the earliest trees to arrive are pioneer species such as ash, birch and alder. These are fast-growing trees that tolerate a wide range of soils and conditions. Foresters mix them at planting time with the slower climax trees, partly to get a quick cover on a bare site and also to provide temporary shelter for the others, and for this reason they are often called 'nurse trees'.

They are all valuable woodland plants in their own right, but because of their fast growth, airy lightweight canopies that let in plenty of sunlight and, in some cases, their relatively short life, they are usually regarded as expendable once they have established the environment and the later trees are large enough to look after themselves. Conifers are commercially used in mixed woods as nurse trees for broad-leaved species – Corsican pine to protect beech, for example, or European larch and Norway spruce for oaks – but for instant appeal you might prefer to plant a selection of deciduous pioneers.

Birches are great favourites and two particular species are widely used for nursing beech in its early stages. The silver birch (*Betula pendula*) prefers dryish soils, while the other British native, the downy birch (*B. pubescens*) favours wet sites (see page 88). They are both slender, elegant trees that can be planted singly or in a bundle of 4–5 young whips that will develop into an eye-catching multi-stemmed feature. Although short-lived, surviving for only 70–80 years, they are vigorous and can put on 90cm (3ft) or more annually for the first 10–15 years.

Another sprinter is the common alder (*Alnus glutinosa*), a valuable pioneer for damp sites because its roots develop nitrogen-fixing nodules that make their own fertilizer from the atmosphere. While not as graceful as some of its cultivated varieties such as the cut-leaved and golden alders ('Laciniata' and 'Aurea'), the simple species is tough and very hardy, which it needs to be because its flowers appear as early as February. It is often planted as a coppice crop – hard-pruned trees which quickly produce thickets of strong straight poles that used to be harvested for making charcoal.

Ash (*Fraxinus*) might seem a surprising choice for a nurse tree because it can live much longer than other pioneers, and large spreading trees are often found here and there in deciduous woodlands throughout lowland areas of Britain. It grows fast, however, with an open canopy of branches that casts very thin shade, and foliage that appears late in spring, lasting for a relatively short season and therefore favouring plants growing beneath. Its seedlings often fail to germinate or grow unless in full sun, so it is a natural colonizer of open ground, especially deep, slightly alkaline soils that do not dry out too much.

A tree with very similar foliage and branch structure, and an even faster growth rate, is the rowan or mountain ash (*Sorbus aucuparia*), which is sufficiently wind-resistant and acid-tolerant to grow high up in the mountains, but equally happy on all lowland soils except heavy clay. Its slender divided leaves turn brilliant yellow and red before they fall, and it has attractive flattened heads

cuttings

■ Birch is one of the most useful of all trees: it is used in the Scottish Highlands for thatching houses, the wood is used to make stools, gates and carts, the bark for tanning leather, manufacturing rope and, when twisted, as candles, and the sap is used to make wine and smoke hams.

■ Dogwood, the common name for *Cornus*, is hardly glamorous, but it has nothing to do with dogs. In fact it comes from *dagwood*, a *dag* being a spike or skewer (hence the word '*dagger*'!), implements that were traditionally made from the straight hard stems.

■ Holly is a hard dense wood, used to make carved butter prints and engraving blocks, and was regarded as the best timber for whip handles, possibly because it was believed to have magical powers over horses.

■ Although ivy appears to smother trees, it is not in fact a parasite and gets nothing from its host except support. It is a valuable woodland plant for wildlife, and the only danger to a tree is the sheer weight of the ivy – and, of course, strangulation!

from left to right Alnus glutinosa (alder), *Betula pendula* (silver birch) and *Sorbus aucuparia* (mountain ash).

of white flowers followed by bright scarlet berries, so you might want to keep it as a feature rather than as a temporary nurse tree. Equally happy on poor, preferably acid soils, the aspen (*Populus tremula*) grows very fast in situations where there is no overhead shade. Its toothed rounded leaves have long delicate stalks that move in the slightest breeze, so the whole tree trembles and rustles with a soft distinctive voice.

All these are simple native species and, as often happens, there are cultivated forms and species from elsewhere that you might feel have more appeal in garden surroundings. For example, a whole range of birches are available from North America and the Far East, most retaining the pioneer qualitites that nurse trees need combined with a more ornamental appearance. One of the best is the Himalayan birch (*Betula utilis*) which has a diaphanous canopy and burnished orange- or copper-brown bark that peels like sun-burnt skin, or there is its Kashmir cousin, *B. u.* var. *jacquemontii*, with brilliant white bark, especially in the variety 'Silver Shadow' – this has the purest, dazzling white bark of all, and actually appears to glow in the evening light.

Decorative relatives of other pioneer species include the award-winning alder *Alnus glutinosa* 'Imperialis', a more slender version of the cut-leaved alder, with a graceful relaxed shape and finely divided leaves, and the fast-growing Italian alder (*A. cordata*), which is tall, shapely and very hardy despite its Mediterranean origins. *Fraxinus americana*, the white ash, has slender vigorous growth and pretty foliage, especially in the form 'Autumn Purple', which has rich autumn tints. Among the many garden forms of the mountain ash, the cut-leaved *Sorbus aucuparia* 'Aspleniifolia' and yellow-berried var. *xanthocarpa* are outstanding.

Virtually all the rowans are renowned for their autumn colours, but for a really stunning display it is hard to beat the sweet gum (*Liquidambar styraciflua*). Attractive even in summer and often giving the tree the superficial appearance of an acer (although I think its shape and habit are superior), its foliage is second to none in autumn, blazing in shades of amber, lemon, crimson and copper. Not as fast-growing as some of the other pioneer species, it is still useful in this respect and too glamorous to omit from this selection.

For something a little more exotic the Persian ironwood (*Parrotia persica*) from northern Iran has some of the finest autumn colour of all. It needs plenty of space, especially in warmer gardens where it can reach 10m (33ft) or more as a large tree on a single trunk with delicately peeling bark like that of a London plane tree, but if required it can be grown as a large shrub in smaller gardens by cutting it back occasionally. It has the reputation of producing the deepest crimson leaf tints of any species, and makes a particularly exciting pioneer on very alkaline soils.

climax trees

Following on from all these as components of the uppermost forest layer are climax species such as oak and beech. Sometimes called 'emergent' species for the simple reason that they are the ones that finally emerge from the top of the woodland canopy – they establish and grow over a much longer period of time, and as many of the pioneer trees come to the end of their lives the climax trees take over in a natural succession. They are long-term competitors that might need some careful nursing at first, but in the end one or another will become the predominant species (which one depends on soil type and altitude) found in most of the mature woods and copses we see all around in the countryside.

In the wild the Scots pine (*Pinus sylvestris*) is the foremost natural conifer species of upland forests in northern Europe, its native territory stretching right across Siberia almost to the Pacific. Although in the vanguard of advancing trees returning to Britain as the ice sheet withdrew northwards thousands of years ago, and for a while, the predominant forest species throughout Britain, it is now confined to the highlands of Scotland. It is a tall strong tree that can withstand both drought and occasional water-logging, but it is very vulnerable while young to prolonged frost and rodent damage, and benefits from the protection of nurse trees if it is to grow with a straight, uninjured main stem.

Oaks are the trees that come to mind when most people think of woods, but not everyone realizes there are two distinct native species. The sessile oak (*Quercus petraea*), so called because the stalkless acorns appear to be sitting (hence 'sessile') on the twigs, was the first to arrive and colonize the thawing land. It is usually found wild in mountains and on well-drained or acid soils, and makes a handsome tree with a tall straight trunk that only branches at the top. The English, common or pedunculate oak (*Q. robur*) with acorns on slender stalks, is the kind foresters like to plant because it grows much faster when young. It thrives in heavy clay and alkaline soils, and develops into an irregular, short-stemmed branching tree, the kind you expect to see when you visit a famous old oak.

Both are worth planting in large gardens and become very densely populated with wildlife – they can support over 280 different insect species, which compares well with, say, the 60 species that live on beech and only 3–4 on a yew or walnut. If your oak trees start to get too large for their space, you can always coppice them down to ground level or pollard them to a height of 90cm–1.8m (3–6ft), after which they will throw up new branches that you can harvest as useful poles after a few years. During that time, the sunlight you have let in by cutting down the overhead canopy will stimulate a lot of ground layer plants to grow and flower, as happens in the wild whenever a tree dies and falls.

from top to bottom *Liquidambar styraciflua* (sweet gum) and *Fagus sylvatica* (beech).

from top to bottom *Larix decidua* (European larch) and *Acer platinoides* (Norway maple).

Beech (*Fagus sylvatica*) is the other great deciduous woodland tree, happy on alkaline soils and quickly producing a canopy that casts shade so dense that most other species are suppressed – these include oak, one of the reasons why the two trees are rarely found together. On its own, beech usually branches low and grows into a spreading tree with large boughs that can reach right down to the ground, but in woods, where space is tight, it produces tall straight trunks that start branching near the top of the emergent layer. At various times of year beeches shed huge quantities of flowers, leaf-bud cases, twigs, leaves and seeds (beech mast), so it is not a tree for tidy gardeners, but all this debris quickly rots down into a thick layer of rich leaf-mould, making it an excellent species for improving poor soils. The flowers and fresh leaves are vulnerable to spring frosts and cold winds, so young beech should be protected by nurse trees or a windbreak until they are larger, and they are not trees to grow in frost pockets. You can trim thin shoots to shape, but coppicing is rarely successful.

The wild cherry (*Prunus avium*) grows fast, especially where exposed to plenty of light, so it can be used as a pioneer or nurse species, but it eventually makes a forest tree of 25m (80ft) or more and is an effective climax species in the absence of other, more dominant trees like oak or beech. It can even survive light dappled shade as an understorey tree, making it a versatile choice. In spring it is a froth of pure white blossom, followed (where more than one specimen is grown) by heavy crops of small, reddish-black cherries that are sometimes sweet enough to gather for cooking or turning into wine, if you can get there before the birds. It has handsome red-brown bark that peels off mature trees in large horizontal sheets, and if felled or coppiced produces clumps of young shoots and suckers that can develop into dense thickets. Its leaves turn yellow, orange and deep red in autumn, especially on more acid soils.

With the exception of the fast-growing wild cherry, you may never see these climax trees reach their full height, of course, but the nature of gardening is to lay down the seeds for the next generation and there is a deep satisfaction in planting something so long-lasting that it will give pleasure decades hence. There are many garden forms of these trees, together with alternative species, that you might prefer to plant for more immediate amenity value and still manage to build an impressive climax canopy that will in time satisfy all the key criteria of a mature woodland.

There is a general feeling that conifers might be acceptable as nurse trees, but only the Forestry Commission would plant them deliberately as climax trees and the rest of us should avoid the 'plantation' look by growing deciduous broad-leaved species. Conifers have their place, however, especially on high or steep ground, and can look magnificent over-topping a canopy of deciduous foliage. Some of the more ornamental or shapely species have plenty of appeal far beyond the popular conception of a conifer as a plain green Christmas tree.

The grand or giant fir (*Abies grandis*), for example, is a pleasing, conical-shaped narrow tree that looks handsome as a solitary specimen, but can be even more impressive as part of a small group or when grown alone within a mixed wood. One of the tallest trees in the world, it is reasonably quick-growing, although slower than the nurse trees and able to benefit at first from their shelter. Often painfully slow to start, this North American native will put on 1–1.5m (3–5ft) annually after the first 5–6 years, and has been known to grow 50m (165ft) in 40 years. In its homeland 90–100m (300–330ft) has been recorded, but don't panic – it is usually much shorter in gardens. In winter its frost-laden silhouette would grace any Christmas card, and its needles have a wonderful fruity fragrance of orange peel. It is certainly a species to consider if you have the space.

If you enjoy eating pine nuts, then you could try the Italian stone pine (*Pinus pinea*), perhaps the best of several kinds grown for their seeds. Although a Mediterranean species, it is very hardy and one of the few pines to succeed on chalky soils. With its reddish-orange bark and broad spreading canopy, it is a very arresting tree and a woodland group would make a memorable feature. Its foliage is blue-green for the first 5–10 years, after which it becomes dark green and the first cones start to appear – these take three years to ripen if you are seriously thinking of cropping them. The deciduous maidenhair tree (*Ginkgo biloba*) and evergreen monkey puzzle (*Araucaria araucana*) both produce edible seeds and several of either would make a fine woodland stand – in some areas of Chile, whole forests are composed of monkey puzzles.

Larches are deciduous conifers with a lot of good qualities to commend them, so it is surprising that they are seldom planted in gardens. They grow fast and are popular as nurse trees and shelter belts, but the European larch (*Larix decidua*) can attain 18m (60ft) in 18 years, which qualifies it as a climax tree. It stands out in early spring, when it shines with its rosy pink flowers, followed quickly by the freshest green foliage, which turns golden yellow in autumn. The open, drooping canopy casts little shade and this, together with the carpet of falling leaves, encourages bluebells and other woodland flowers to thrive beneath.

One of the last trees to get through before the land bridge with the rest of Europe disappeared was the hornbeam (*Carpinus betulus*), which is one of the best deciduous trees for planting on clay where it was often grown as pollards for crops of strong, hard poles. Remnants of these ancient forests can still be seen around London to this day. A hornbeam wood can make an interesting change from the classic beech woodland – both look rather similar and produce a neat, deep green canopy that is well worth waiting for. In autumn its leaves, rather like those of beech but deeply ribbed, turn yellow and then a deep brown, not so burnished as beech but still attractive. Growing slowly to 30m (100ft), it can be cut back if necessary according to traditional practice.

The field maple (*Acer campestre*), the only native British maple, is just one of many acers that can be used as climax trees. It is happiest in hedgerows and small woods on chalk and limestone, where it grows – quickly at first, but later slowing down – into a strong, good-looking 15m (50ft) tree with a straight trunk and broad, domed crown. Watch out for its autumn tints, ranging from clear yellow to deep orange. For clay, thin chalky soils and even acid sandstone, a better choice might be the Norway maple (*Acer platanoides*), which is one of the fastest growing species, often increasing by 2m (6ft) per year. Spectacular in spring when covered with yellow-green bunches of blossom, it has another season in autumn when its foliage turns brilliant soft yellow.

Various kinds of crab or wild apples are found in hedges, copses and the lighter edges of large woods. The true crab (*Malus sylvestris*) is relatively small, just 8m (26ft) high, but would be large enough for grouping in a smaller garden as the main climax tree. Many wild apples, however, are seedlings from culti-vated varieties and may be much larger, just as your favourite eating apple can be if grown on the most vigorous rootstock. An orchard of large apple trees might seem a very tame substitute for the true wild wood, but all the same prin-ciples apply and you could combine these with an understorey of shrubs – whether fruiting kinds or native wild species – and a ground layer of wild flowers, producing a successful blend of forest garden and natural woodland.

shrub and scrub

As I've hinted several times already, a woodland is much more than just a succession or collection of trees. These only form the canopy, which may be the layer you first see from afar, but the plants that flourish beneath are as rich, important and diverse as those growing above.

When an area of forest first begins to emerge, nurse tree seedlings develop along with sun-loving herbaceous and shrubby plants, competing for the same sunlight and nutrients, but as the trees mature the smaller plants are increas-ingly shaded by the developing canopy and eventually die in the declining light levels. The wood will now be colonized by increasing numbers of shade-loving plants, which relish conditions in this new habitat where sunlight is rationed, whether in quality or according to the season – high light levels in winter can dwindle to relative gloom by mid-summer in a mature deciduous wood. The result is a rich and varied flora, from delicate bulbs to glossy-leaved shrubs, that is totally reliant on the tree canopy above to sustain the right growing conditions.

One of the first shrubs to appear and thrive in both the early sunlit period and the later, more established shade is the familiar elder or elderberry (*Sambucus nigra*). Its height varies according to the amount of light it receives, and it can range from a short shrub little more than 1.2m (4ft) high to a branching 10m (33ft) tree. Succeeding in most soils but happiest on alkaline or fertile ground, it produces broad heads of fragrant creamy-white flowers in early summer, followed by heavy clusters of round black fruits, loved by wine-makers and birds everywhere – in fact, this undemanding plant can be an effective decoy in orchards, tempting birds away from ripening apples. Don't bother buying plants: simply locate one in the wild with the sweetest flower scent or heaviest fruit crops, take a few hardwood cuttings in autumn, and you should have 100% success.

One deciduous understorey shrub easily propagated from hardwood cuttings or from seed – which is the way birds have spread it throughout most of Europe – is the common dogwood (*Cornus sanguinea*). This is a lime-lover that thrives in dappled (but not dense) shade, especially in the predominantly ash woodlands of fertile uplands. Its distinctive red-tinted stems sucker freely, eventually forming dense thickets that may conceal many small birds' nests and look particularly good in winter. Add to this its flat heads of white flowers and black pea-sized berries, and you have a shrub for all seasons.

A familiar hedging species that actually grows wild as a scrub and understorey plant where the shade is not too dense, common hawthorn (*Crataegus monogyna*) will also grow into a shapely 15m (50ft) tree if left to its own devices. It is thorny and branches prolifically, qualities that make it a good intruder-proof choice for hedges and windbreaks round garden woodlands, and its sweetly fragrant flowers (May blossom) and brilliant crimson fruits (haws) will add spectacular flushes of colour to your planting scheme. It grows virtually anywhere except on poor acid soils, but on heavy clay you are more likely to find its close cousin *C. laevigata*, the Midland hawthorn. Examples of this in the wild are generally thought to be relics of ancient woodland, so it might be the species to choose if you are recreating a really authentic traditional wood.

from top to bottom *Sambucus nigra* (elder) and *Ilex aquifolum* (common holly).

Probably the commonest evergreen understorey shrub is holly, often concentrated in thickets all round large oaks, where birds originally perched and dropped the seeds. The common holly (*Ilex aquifolium*) can tolerate the densest shade, its long whippy shoots arching down to the ground where they root and spread the clump in all directions. Its leaves are rich glossy green, spiny at low levels as a defence against browsers and often quite smooth higher up the plants. The flowers are single-sexed and you need both male and female plants

from left to right *Rosa canina* (dog rose), *Buxus sempervirens* (box) and *Daphne laureola* (spurge laurel).

to produce berries, the best crops of which are borne after a hot summer. It grows on most soils, usually as a shrub up to 10m (33ft) high, although you can prune it much lower, but where there is light and space it will make a sturdy climax tree of twice that height or more.

Twining and looping through and between these shrubs are the briars and brambles, the thorny suckering blackberries and roses that use their hooked spines to haul themselves up into whatever light is available. Where the shade is densest, they produce large leaves and few flowers or fruit, but in small sunny clearings they can be lush and productive, attracting bees and butterflies from all around. The wild blackberry or bramble (*Rubus fruticosus* agg.) favours drier soils, whereas dog roses (*Rosa canina*) and the very similar field rose (*R. arvensis*) prefer heavy ground that is consistently moist all summer. Any or all of these would look right in controlled patches in your natural wood, or you could replace them without spoiling the overall effect with a cultivated black-berry such as the robust 'Himalayan Giant' or unarmed 'Oregon Thornless', which can be partnered with one or two rambler rose varieties.

There are probably more shade-loving garden species for the understorey zone than many of us appreciate. These tend to be sun-worshippers, but nestling underneath the lush canopy of tree foliage in the lightly shaded wood-land is a whole new, gentler world of plants reliant on the environment created by the trees to protect them from sunburn and wind-scorch.

Commonest of these, at least where the soil is neutral or alkaline, is the hazel, (*Corylus avellana*), a multi-stemmed large shrub or small tree that can produce open thickets of soft green foliage and bagfuls of nuts, if the squirrels don't get them first!. It is an excellent choice for the woodland garden. Leave it to make a huge 10m (33ft) feature dripping with golden catkins in early spring,clip it as a marginal hedge, coppice the branches every 5–7 years for runner bean poles, or cut it more often for the thinner twiggy stems that make the best pea sticks. The plain species is a refreshing shade of green, or you might prefer the purple-leaved filbert (*C. maxima* 'Purpurea'). The golden hazel (*C. a.* 'Aurea') needs sun and will turn a sour green in woodland shade, while the ever-popular corkscrew hazel or 'Harry Lauder's walking-stick' (*C. a.* 'Contorta') looks distinctly odd in a wood and is best reserved for a patio oddity.

Better known as a clipped topiary species for formal gardens, common box (*Buxus sempervirens*) is a native of British woodlands, especially in the milder south where it thrives on dryish alkaline soils. It grows slowly into a spreading shrub up to 5m (16ft) tall, but do not be put off by its size because it is easily cut back if it sprawls too far. The distinctive, tiny glossy leaves will give your planting scheme evergreen structure all year round, as will spurge laurel (*Daphne laureola*), another lime-loving evergreen with leathery shiny leaves and upright branching stems about 90cm (3ft) high. The cornelian cherry (*Cornus mas*) is a fine naturalized deciduous shrub or small tree that flowers in late winter, long before its leaves open, and was once cultivated for its scarlet, sour plum-flavoured berries. Although it can reach 5m (16ft) on woodland edges, you can keep it trimmed much shorter as a low scrub plant.

For acid soils, gaultherias are spreading, sometimes suckering shrubs that like a little moisture while young but become drought-tolerant once established. The salal (*Gaultheria shallon*) produces sweet, edible purple berries and grows like an evergreen carpet, just 15cm (6in) high, whereas the wintergreen or checkerberry (*G. procumbens*) makes a 1.5m (5ft) clump of long, deep green leaves and scarlet berries that attract birds from far and wide.

Finally, don't forget the various climbers that will enjoy meandering through the shrubs or creeping up tree trunks to drape the branches with a curtain of foliage, flowers and fruits. Grape vines are natural woodland plants, preferring the margins where they get sun for part of each day but are near the woody hosts they need for support (in Italy they are regularly trained into trees). With their broad maple-like leaves, these are some of the most ornamental climbers you could choose and, if you are lucky, you might get enough fruit to make them a profitable asset. In colder gardens, *Vitis* 'Brant' is the most likely to produce fruit, but there are many other outdoor varieties suitable for milder districts, especially seedless kinds such as 'Sultana' or 'Perlette'.

The most typical climbers for woodland habitats are the twiners, plants such as wild honeysuckle and traveller's joy, which wrap their long sinuous stems round every available branch in their perpetual scramble for light. Sun-lovers they might be, but they relish having their roots and lower growth in cool shade. Do not plant them on new trees – their rampant shoots might smother and cripple the young tree shoots, but you can safely grow them on more established hosts. Traveller's joy or old man's beard (*Clematis vitalba*) is the more vigorous

cuttings

■ **Leave foxglove flowers to set seed, up to 2 million of which are produced in a single flower spike. Once the seedlings have germinated, gently lift them and move them to new positions or simply thin them where they grow to about 15cm (6in) apart.**

■ **Wild garlic or ramsons has been used to cure just about every illness, from leprosy and smallpox to asthma and whooping cough, but its origin was thought to be more sinister, for it was said to have sprung up in the place where Satan's foot fell as he walked out of Eden.**

■ **When the fresh root of Solomon's seal was dug up and crushed, it was used to treat bruises, removing their ugly colour after one or two nights. It was also said to work on piles, but neither of these uses is reliable!**

■ **The last part of the wild blackberry's name, *Rubus fruticosus* agg., is short for *aggregatus*, a reference to the fact that botanists cannot agree if there are over 280 different species of this variable plant or just numerous subtle variations of one.**

from top to bottom *Digitalis purpurea* (foxglove), *Galanthus nivalis* (snowdrop) and *Polygonatum multiflorum* (Solomon's seal).

of the two, easily soaring to 30m (100ft) and draping trees in cascades of leafy shoots, greenish-cream flowers and feathery fruits. It prefers alkaline soils, unlike wild honeysuckle or woodbine (*Lonicera periclymenum*) which prefers acid conditions. Although more restrained, this can still climb up to 6m (20ft), producing its perfumed red and creamy-yellow blooms all summer, followed by red fleshy berries that spangle the trees with brilliantly coloured highlights.

bulbs and herbaceous plants

The most prolific source of colour is the lowest planting layer, the ground level plants that crave the gentle light. There is a host of wild flowers (and suitable garden substitutes) for these situations, and many are 'indicator' plants, slow to establish naturally into large colonies and therefore used by ecologists to identify an ancient wood. These include wood sorrel, dog's mercury, sweet woodruff, ramsons or wild garlic, herb Paris and lily-of-the-valley.

Best known of these native species is, of course, the bluebell (*Hyacinthoides non-scripta*). Although found in many other parts of Europe, it is commonest in Britain, so much so that it has become almost a woodland emblem. A perennial bulb that flowers and seeds in the soft spring light, it forms dense colonies that spread to carpet the ground with a sea of blue. You can plant them in drifts as bulbs or grow them by gathering and scattering the prolific seeds as soon as these are ripe, but make sure you have the true English species, with drooping flowers on one side of the stalk only. The Spanish bluebell (*H. hispanica*), which has blooms evenly set all round the stalk, is grown in gardens and should stay there, because it is more vigorous and can out-rival its more delicate cousin.

One wild bulb that has no trouble with competition is *Allium ursinum*, the wild garlic or ramsons. Even with your eyes shut, you know these are around just from the pervasive smell of onions. Most allium species like full sun and open positions, but ramsons is a true woodland plant. Its pure white flowers have the same impact as snowdrops when you see them in great drifts, while its broad gleaming leaves cover the ground with a satisfying deep green carpet.

Another lavish mat-forming species, this time a rhizomatous perennial that tends to grow with primroses and wood cranesbill in poor soils, is the wood anemone (*A. nemorosa*). In really old deciduous woodland its nodding blooms will speckle the ground, but it is also at home on mountain tops, where it earns its other common name of windflower. Wood sorrel (*Oxalis acetosella*) is similar in appearance, but its more rounded white or pinkish-white flowers, embroidered with lilac veins, appear a few weeks later than windflowers. The shamrock-like leaves close up at the slightest touch or hint of sunlight, as do the flowers when rain threatens. A few plants will spread rapidly, their seeds scattering as the dry seed-pods crack open.

Some of the loveliest woodland wild-flowers are ancestors of familiar border perennials that have been 'improved' almost beyond recognition. The common columbine (*Aquilegia vulgaris*), for example, is an artless gem of alkaline soils, able to tolerate full sun but in the wild tending to choose dapped shade, where its violet-blue, short-spurred flowers seem more intensely coloured. Its greyish, finely cut foliage is pretty too, particularly in spring when it is tinged with pink

Similarly, the wood cranesbill (*Geranium sylvaticum*) has basal clumps of attractive leaves, resembling ferns, and veined blooms that can look reddish-purple, lilac pink or violet blue according to the light and time of day. Unlike most cranesbills, which are native plants of meadows, this likes the partial shade of woodland edges and hedge bottoms, much the same as its cousin, the mourning widow (*G. phaeum*). The opulent purple-maroon, almost black flowers of this naturalized species from southern Europe produce an arresting early summer display when grouped as ground cover. Their cultivated relatives would look quite out of place in a natural woodland, as would garden forms of the common foxglove (*Digitalis purpurea*). An alternative to the familiar (purple or white) native species is the large yellow foxglove (*D. grandiflora*) which produces 90cm (3ft) spires of almost horizontal pale yellow flowers with fine brown veins. Its leaves are lusher and shinier than the common foxglove's, catching and reflecting the light. The small yellow foxglove, *D. lutea*, is a 60cm (2ft) miniature version, with more slender, paler yellow blooms and narrower leaves.

To add some truly beautiful foliage you could grow Solomon's seal (*Polygonatum multiflorum*). It is an uncommon, local native of dryish British woods, where it is often found on its own. This lonely prominence emphasizes its characteristic feature; long arching stems like fishing rods, strung with tiny greenish-white clusters of waxy bells, each perfectly aligned with a pair of lush green leaves. It will cope with quite deep shade, as can sweet woodruff (*Galium odoratum*), also known as kiss-me-quick. It occurs widely and almost exclusively in forests and deep woods, where its dense heads of tiny, pure white flowers stand out like stars against the background of leaf litter.

Convallaria majalis is another familiar garden plant that belongs in dryish woods rather than well-watered lowlands as its common name, lily-of-the-valley, suggests. Add lungwort (*Pulmonaria officianalis*) and sweet violets (*Viola odorata*), and you would complete a select band of perennials that look much more authentic in a woodland setting than in the open border. Among several bulb species that belong under the trees are the snowdrop, *Galanthus nivalis*, both its common single form and the double 'Flore pleno'.

plants for a woodland garden

nurse trees

Alnus rubra
red alder, Oregon alder
height 25m (80ft).
spread 10m (33ft).
habit Hardy deciduous tree.
season Foliage spring; flowers (catkins) March.
site Full sun, on moist or heavy soils.
characteristics A narrow tree, conical at first and later broad-domed, growing 90cm (3ft) or more annually while young. Bright yellow male catkins, up to 15cm (6in) long, followed by clusters of large barrel-shaped 'cones' that turn brown in autumn. Large oval leaves, bright pink in spring and later deep green.
how to grow Plant while dormant. Prune to maintain shape while young, but do not coppice after 5–6 years old.
note The roots fix atmospheric nitrogen, so it is a good choice for poor soils, and the leaf litter is a rich fertilizer for nearby climax trees.

Hippophae rhamnoides
sea buckthorn
height 10m (33ft).
spread 6m (20ft).
habit Hardy deciduous shrub or small tree.
season Foliage spring–autumn; fruits autumn–winter.
site Full sun, on well-drained light soil.
characteristics A fast-growing pioneer windbreak shrub (or small tree in sheltered spots). It binds loose poor soil with its vigorous nitrogen-fixing roots. Spiny drooping branches bear silvery willow-like leaves and greenish spring flowers, followed by bright orange berries all winter.
how to grow Plant while dormant, one male for every 5–6 females for berry crops. Prune and chop out suckers in winter if invasive.
note The willow-leaved buckthorn (*H. salicifolia*) is less spiny, with pretty leaves and heavy fruit crops, but is not so hardy.

Quercus rubra
(syn. *Q. borealis*) red oak
height 25m (80ft).
spread 18m (60ft).
habit Hardy deciduous tree.
season Foliage autumn; fruits autumn.
site Full sun, on well-drained lime-free soil.
characteristics A straight, fast-growing tree 2.4m (8ft) annually while young), with a spreading shapely crown and smooth greyish bark. The large, spiky lobed leaves on red twigs are deep green, turning vivid yellow, red and copper in autumn.
how to grow Plant while dormant, and stake securely for the first 3–4 years. Prune off lower sideshoots in winter for a clean straight trunk.
note A very wind-resistant North American oak, widely grown as a colourful nurse tree and shelter belt at the edge of conifer forests, but also makes a good climax tree.

climax trees

Nyssa sinensis
Chinese tupelo
height 10m (33ft).
spread 10m (33ft).
habit Hardy slow-growing deciduous large shrub or small tree.
season Foliage autumn.
site Full sun with shelter from cold winds, on deep, well-drained, lime-free soil.
characteristics A multi-stemmed shrub or broadly conical branching tree, with slow thin growth in the early years. The large tapering leaves are reddish-bronze when young and in autumn turn gold, orange, scarlet and crimson.
how to grow Plant small, container-grown specimens while dormant, with support for the first 4–5 years. Keep well-sheltered from cold winds. Prune to maintain a single leading shoot for a shapely tree.
note The tupelo or black gum from North America, (*N. sylvatica*), is much larger, with equally spectacular autumn tints.

Pseudotsuga menziesii
Douglas fir
height 55m (180ft).
spread 7m (23ft).
habit Hardy evergreen coniferous tree.
season Foliage all year.
site Full sun with some shelter at first, on moist, well-drained lime-free soil.
characteristics One of the tallest conifers – 100m (325ft) – it has a straight, fast-growing trunk and blistered, corrugated bark. Slender and conical, with dense dark green foliage, resinously aromatic. Cones are long, light brown with protruding three-pronged bracts.
how to grow Plant in autumn or mid-spring as small plants, with shelter to prevent wind damage to the leading shoot. As trees grow, prune all lower sideshoots to leave a 3m (10ft) clean trunk.
note Give the trees plenty of sun to discourage aphids. The timber is well-known to carpenters as 'Oregon pine'.

Prunus avium 'Plena'
double wild cherry
height 12m (40ft)
spread 10–12m (33–40ft).
habit Hardy deciduous tree.
season Foliage autumn; flowers May; fruit mid-summer.
site Full sun, in moist well-drained soil.
characteristics A large broad tidy tree with a dense spreading canopy and mahogany bark. Very double, pure white flowers open with the new foliage, which turns yellow, orange and crimson in autumn. The prolific red fruits are usually eaten by birds before they turn black.
how to grow Plant while dormant and stake for the first 2–3 years in exposed sites. Prune (summer only to avoid diseases) to keep a single leading stem.
note The single-flowered *P. avium* or gean is the ancestor of most cultivated cherry varieties and is used as a rootstock for grafting larger trees.

Hippophae rhamnoides (sea buckthorn)

Quercus rubra (red oak)

Nyssa sinensis (Chinese tupelo)

Prunus avium 'Plena' (double wild cherry)

shrub and scrub

Cornus alba
red-barked dogwood
height 3m (10ft).
spread 3m (10ft).
habit Hardy deciduous
shrub.
season Foliage autumn;
flowers May–June;
bark winter.
site Full sun or light
shade, in any soil.
characteristics Thickets
of vigorous red-barked
stems (yellow or green in
some cultivars), and oval
dark green leaves that turn
orange and rich red in
autumn. Flat heads of
white or yellowish-green
flowers are followed by
off-white berries tinged
with blue. The bright red
young shoots are a winter
feature.
how to grow Plant while
dormant, 60–90cm (2–3ft)
apart in groups. Prune
stems hard in early April
for bright stem colour.
note An excellent
screening plant, so could
be used as a marginal
hedge or pioneer shrub to
nurse small trees.

Nandina domestica
heavenly bamboo
height 1.8m (6ft).
spread 1.5m (5ft).
habit Hardy evergreen or
semi-evergreen shrub.
season Foliage spring and
autumn; flowers July;
fruits August–winter.
site Full sun or very light
shade with shelter from
cold winds, in moist
well-drained soil.
characteristics An upright
multi-stemmed shrub, with
long elegant leaves divided
into leaflets – usually
evergreen, but semi-
evergreen in cold winters.
The foliage is red-tinted in
spring, and fiery orange-
red and purple in autumn.
Large panicles of small
star-shaped flowers are
followed in a hot summer
by bright red fruits.
how to grow Plant in
autumn or mid-spring.
Prune large plants in
spring, cutting out one
branch in three.
note Hard winter frosts
can kill top growth, but
plants revive from the base.

Symphoricarpos albus
var. laevigatus
(syn. S. rivularis)
snowberry
height 1.8m (6ft).
spread 1.8m (6ft)
or more.
habit Hardy deciduous
suckering shrub.
season Fruits autumn
and winter.
site Full sun to dense
shade, in any soil.
characteristics An
indestructible vigorous
shrub forming thickets
of tall arching stems,
with large oval dark green
leaves. Tiny pink bell-
shaped flowers are
followed by round fruits.
how to grow Plant while
dormant and then cut back
hard to encourage
branching. Trim back
suckers in winter if they
are invasive, and remove
one branch in three from
older congested plants.
note No one wants this
snowberry in a formal
shrubbery, but its
wayward suckering habit
is ideal for a woodland.

bulbs and herbaceous plants

Erythronium oregonum
dog's-tooth violet
height 30–45cm
(12–18in).
spread 10–13cm (4–5in).
habit Hardy bulbous
perennial.
season Flowers
April–May.
site Partial shade, in
moist well-drained soil.
characteristics Vigorous,
clump-forming plant, with
broad shiny deep green
leaves mottled with liver-
coloured spots. Up to 6–7
long-stemmed pendent
creamy-white flowers.
Plants resent disturbance
and drying out if out of
the ground.
how to grow Plant in
autumn 10cm (4in) deep
and 8cm (3in) apart in
groups. Leave to spread
until clumps are over-
crowded. Divide these in
August and then replant.
note E. californicum is
similar: the white or
pink-flowered European
species, E. dens-canis,
is not native, but is happy
in shade or full sun.

Geum urbanum
wood avens, herb bennet,
cloveroot
height 60cm (2ft).
spread 30cm (12in).
habit Hardy herbaceous
rhizomatous perennial.
season Flowers
June–August.
site Full or semi-shade,
in any fertile soil.
characteristics A hairy
plant, forming a mat of
toothed and deeply-lobed
dark green leaves, with
strong branching stems
bearing a succession of
small bright yellow flowers
that droop as they age and
mature into feathery seed
clusters. Roots are short
thick clove-scented
rhizomes. Usually found in
oak and oak-ash woods.
how to grow Sow in situ
in spring or autumn, or
plant 15cm (6in) apart.
note If grown near
moisture-loving water
avens (G. rivale) many
hybrid seedlings can
appear with a mixture
of their parents'
characteristics.

Helleborus niger
Christmas rose
height 30cm (12in).
spread 45cm (18in).
habit Hardy herbaceous
perennial with
over-wintering foliage.
season Flowers
January–March.
site Dappled shade, in
moist neutral or alkaline
soil.
characteristics Basal
clumps of leathery, dark
green leaves divided into
numerous leaflets. Strong
purple stems bear 8cm
(3in) saucer-shaped
blooms, single or in small
clusters and gleaming
waxy-white with green
centres.
how to grow Add plenty
of leaf-mould to the site,
and plant in spring 30cm
(12in) apart. Keep watered
in dry weather during the
first year, shelter from cold
winds, and mulch with
leaf-mould the next spring.
note This is a Central
European species, but
H. viridis and H. foetidus
are native to British woods
on alkaline soil.

Cornus alba (red-barked dogwood)

Nandina domestica (heavenly bamboo)

Symphoricarpos albus var. *laevigatus*
(snowberry)

Hellborus niger (Christmas rose)

a season

in the natural woodland garden

Woodlands need the minimum of care and the secret of success is to do as little as possible! It is easy to interfere, frightening off wildlife and spoiling the natural balanced cycle of growth, ageing and decay that fuels life in the woods. Clear away fallen branches, rake up autumn leaves or organize self-set seedlings into formal patches, and you could turn a charming wild-wood into a miniature parkland, defeating all your initial efforts to produce a cameo of a natural landscape.

Possibly the most important and exacting task of the year is planting the trees in the first place. This can seem intimidating if you have never done it before, but there is no need for apprehension – it is exactly the same technique as you would use for any shrub or perennial and, like them, trees have a built-in urge to grow, so they are on your side.

For best results, go and see your trees before buying and choose those most likely to develop in a natural way. Very often, nurserymen trim the tops of young trees to encourage early branching low down, whereas yours will need to be strong upright plants with an intact central leading shoot for upward growth. Foresters generally use small bare-rooted seedlings, which they plant by making slits in the ground with a spade, dropping in the seedlings and firming them with their boot, hardly pausing as they walk across the site.

In the garden woodland, you can get faster results by choosing container-grown trees about 90cm–1.8m (3–6ft) high, planting these in previously cultivated positions with stakes for support. It's a little more involved, but gives you a couple of years' head-start. To plant one of these, fork over about a square metre of ground and then, in the centre of the patch, dig a hole at least twice the size of the pot the tree is growing in. Loosen the sides of the hole and add a couple of forkfuls of well-rotted organic matter to the bottom. Remove the pot, place the tree in the hole and backfill with the excavated soil, pressing it firmly into place with the sole of your boot several times as you go.

Firm planting is vital to protect the tree from wind-rock. Before its roots have a good hold on the earth, strong winds can shake the tree, loosening its footing and allowing pockets of air to develop around the roots, so increasing the risk of frost damage. To help it through these first few vulnerable years, stake it securely, but not with a vertical pole as tall as the trunk. Instead drive a shorter stake into the ground immediately after planting, at an angle of about 45 degrees so that the point misses the roots and the top finishes up close to the tree, about one-third of the way up its trunk. Attach the two together with an adjustable tree tie, and check annually that this is not too tight as the trunk swells. The stake can usually be removed after 3–4 years, when the trunk is sturdy and the roots well settled in.

spring

tidying invasive plants – Wild roses and blackberries do not need annual pruning in the same way as their cultivated forms elsewhere in the garden, but they are territorial plants that can sprawl and layer themselves into inconvenient places, especially across paths. Before life returns to the woodland, some time during February perhaps, check round to see if there is a little too much of this spiny ground cover and cut back the straggliest stems to leave clear access between the trees. Where some of the long pliable stems have rooted them-selves, you can sever them and dig them up with a spade for transplanting elsewhere. While you are at it, use the spade to chop out invasive runners and suckers of other shrubs that might be threatening more precious plantings of wild flowers.

planting – There is still time to introduce a few new ground layer plants and even one or two container-grown shrubs, but be prepared to water them regu-larly in a dry summer. Bulbs such as snowdrops, cyclamen and winter aconites are sometimes available 'in the green' (as growing plants in pots), either before flowering or, even better, soon afterwards, when they will settle in quickly without any check to their growth. Although a lot more expensive than buying dry bulbs in autumn (some of which may not grow), planting in the green allows you to position and see the plants instantly in the right place. When you take the bulbs out of the pot, do not be tempted to tease them apart, because most bulbs dis-like disturbance while they are growing. If you need to divide them, wait until they are dormant in mid-summer before digging up and separating clumps.

mulching – Although the ground beneath the tree canopy will be shaded, it is not necessarily moist. Trees can be demanding, absorbing all the available moisture and nutrients from far around, leaving the shrubs, herbaceous

The woodland floor can be a truly vibrant place, bursting with foliage and flower.

perennials and bulbs to grow in dry poor earth. You can compensate for this by mulching around the plants of the lower layers with a thick layer of leaf litter or well-decayed compost in the early spring. As with all mulches, there is no need to dig the litter in because soil invertebrates will gradually carry the organic material into the soil, improving its texture and increasing nutrient levels. Accelerate the development of the new habitat by mulching plants with leaf litter gathered from an established wood, which will often import useful seeds and insects that all contribute to the well-being and diversity of your woodland garden.

summer

paths – A wood is a more complex and interactive eco-system than the other types we are looking at, and will provide a home for all kinds of creatures, most of whom will be at their busiest in the summer. Remember you are sharing the place with them and try wherever possible not to disturb them. For example, do not carry out any major changes or maintenance between March and August, when birds and animals are nesting and raising their young. They could be anywhere – a tree creeper living behind a flap of tree bark, a warbler family just 30cm (12in) above ground in a thicket of brambles, or a family of mice under a simple heap of twigs and prunings. To be safe, make one or two paths through your wood, and keep to these during this critical period.

All paths and other means of access through the woodland should be kept as natural as possible – no paving stones, concrete or brightly painted timber! I suggest marking out a simple informal, meandering path through the wood, made from an underlay of horticultural membrane with a thick layer of bark chippings over the top. This woody material will blend in naturally with the surroundings and also deaden your footfalls if you want to explore and find out what everyone else is up to, which is irresistible in an established wood! Try keeping a diary of all you see, and you will be surprised how quickly some species appreciate the new habitat and all it has to offer.

As August draws to a close, you can re-start any essential care, but always check first for late broods of nestlings. Deciduous woodland hedges and windbreaks, especially those made from hawthorn, beech, hornbeam and field maple, can be trimmed now if they are becoming too tall and overgrown. Don't clip them too neatly unless your wood has a formal edge. Simply prune off the longest shoots with secateurs or loppers, and roughly shear back the sides where growth is expanding too far – into a path, for example, or over special groups of herbaceous plants.

weeding – Although any distinction between a weed and a wild flower can become a little blurred in a woodland context, there are times when you need to subtly intervene in the natural processes of succession and establishment. This might be to protect young plants while they are still susceptible to competition or simply to prevent unwelcome thugs from intruding and taking over, which they can do rapidly during summer.

In a new woodland, young trees get away fastest if they are kept clear of rival plants until they are about 1.5–1.8m (5–6ft) tall. Surround them at planting time with a metre-square mat of woven planting fabric to suppress weeds or check every few months that none have invaded their space. In fact, some gardeners will allow nothing to grow near new trees until a few seasons of natural leaf fall have allowed a layer of ground litter to build up. You can leave a handful of choice wild flowers or even sow one or two species, but most other volunteer plants should be removed while small, especially more persistent kinds such as thistles, ivy and sycamore seedlings.

autumn

If you think that a garden has nothing to entice you outside once all the flowers have faded and the outside temperature drops below 10°C (50°F), then a woodland scheme will certainly change your mind. For deciduous plants the end of the growing season is signalled by autumn's drop in temperature. Dormancy is on the horizon and the photosynthesis that has sustained green growth ceases.

As a result, leaves start to lose their green pigment before they die, and in the process reveal the many different colours beneath that have until now been masked by the green chlorophyll. Shades from butter yellow to blood red will begin to blaze across the garden, accompanied by shining stems of white or burgundy and frost-embroidered seed-heads sparkling in the late sunshine. Autumn is definitely the most exciting time in a woodland garden.

planting – It is also the best time for planting, while the soil is still warm and the weather relatively mild, which allows disturbed roots to make enough new growth to absorb food and water before winter. Deciduous tree and shrub species can be planted from September, just before they start shedding their leaves, right through the winter (whenever conditions are not too cold or wet) until March, but the sooner you begin the better. Evergreens are never fully dormant, but have strong growth spurts in autumn and mid-spring, which are the best times for planting them.

As a rule of thumb, plant trees about 2–3 m (6½–10 ft) apart, although for very speedy development you can reduce this to 1.2m (4ft) if you are prepared to sacrifice some nurse trees fairly early or coppice them after about 5 years.

The woodlands in winter can be starkly beautiful and atmospheric.

Shrubs and herbaceous plants should be planted in natural groups using odd numbers of plants – one for a specimen shrub, for example, and three, five or seven for herbaceous plants. If you use even numbers your brain will automatically divide the plants into their individual components, whereas odd numbers are more easily seen as a single group.

You can also plant most spring-flowering bulbs now. Use hundreds (buy them wholesale, it will be much cheaper) and you will be rewarded with a carpet of colour. They need the same informal approach as herbaceous plants so simply take a handful and scatter them gently in the area where they are to go and then plant each bulb where it falls to create a natural-looking drift.

trees and shrubs from seed – The quickest ways to introduce plants to your woodland is to buy them from a nursery or garden centre, or take hardwood cuttings now and root these in a sheltered piece of ground. The trouble with both these methods is that cuttings simply replicate the donor plant, while growers propagate from a few carefully selected stock plants. Either way you do not get the genetic diversity that occurs in the wild, where most plants start from open-pollinated seed. This helps maintain the subtle differences that prevent all plants from looking alike or succumbing to the same diseases.

Although raising from seed takes a little longer, you can grow a wider range of plants very cheaply, and it is much more exciting than simply buying a plant and popping it in! Autumn is the time to collect ripe seeds from nearby woodlands, and these are best sown straight away. Leave them exposed to frost and rain over winter, and many will germinate the moment temperatures start to rise.

bird boxes – If you already have a forest of your own or just one or two larger trees, consider making a few bird boxes to encourage various woodland species to nest there. You can use scraps and off-cuts of untreated wood to make a range of boxes at various heights to suit the species you have or want to attract. Install them before the winter so that the birds can use them for shelter and get used to their presence.

winter

tidying – With all our conventional training in herbaceous borders it is very tempting to be tidy and clear away dead and dying growth. In a woodland garden, however, it is essential to leave at least some debris lying around to allow the fragile relationships between the plants, insects, fungi and animals to exist. The top growth of herbaceous plants should be left intact over winter, only cutting it down to the crown if necessary in spring. If you do trim it off, just leave it all lying on the woodland floor. Bulbs need to die back completely to allow the goodness from the foliage to return to the bulb and fuel next year's display.

Shrubs and trees will only need the minimum of work. If a limb breaks or is interfering with a path, you can remove it by first cutting off the main weight about 50–60cm (20–24in) from the trunk. Then use a sharp pruning saw to make a small under-cut near the trunk, and finally cut downwards to meet this cut so that the stub is trimmed off cleanly. Any branches that have fallen or been removed can be left lying on the ground (where the rotting material will provide food and homes for a host of fungi, mosses and insects) or piled up in layers to provide a snug shelter for small creatures like mice, voles and toads.

When the canopy becomes too dense you can let in more light by coppicing the nurse trees or understorey woody plants, cutting all their branches to a low stump that will regenerate over the following seasons (see page 99). Species that respond well include ash, alder, birch, elder, hazel, holly, hornbeam and oak. Doing so will stimulate a flush of growth from flowers that have been suppressed by the shade and you could have the best display of bluebells for years! This happens on a larger scale when a mature tree dies. Its demise allows sunlight to flood in, creating a whole new set of conditions in which sun-loving plants, saplings and seedlings will thrive. Only cut down dead trees if they are dangerous. They will decay gracefully, while all around new trees put on rapid growth to restore continuity. Nothing is static here and a year in the woodland garden is just a brief instant in its long evolution. Of all the kinds of natural garden you can make this is the most enduring and, almost certainly, the most satisfying.

cuttings

■ Most deciduous trees and shrubs can be purchased as bare-root plants, grown in the open field and then lifted during the dormant months of October to March. This makes them much less expensive to buy, but you need to plant them soon after purchase, so that the roots are not allowed to dry out.

■ As a general rule, bulbs should be planted two to three times deeper than their length from tip to base. If you are planting snowdrops bought 'in the green' (with growing leaves), make sure you plant them to the same level as they were grown before, keeping the point where the green top growth gives way to the yellow lower part at soil level.

■ If you can gather extra fallen leaves from around the garden or beyond, stuff them into black plastic bags with one or two holes stabbed in the sides; store for a year and you will have a free supply of extra mulching material for your trees. Don't do this with conifer needles though, as they are very acidic and decompose slowly.

■ Most deciduous trees are pruned in late autumn and winter, but some kinds such as *Betula*, *Acer*, *Prunus* and *Aesculus* will exude sap profusely if cut towards the end of winter, and the safest time to prune these is in late summer when growth has matured.

index

credits

BBC Worldwide would like to thank the following for providing photographs and for permission to reproduce copyright material. While every effort has been made to trace and acknowledge all copyright holders, we would like to apologize should there have been any errors or omissions.

A-Z Botanical 8 Adrian Thomas, 30 Anthony Seinet, 32R A Young, 35R Michael R Chandler, 59 Bjorn Svensson, 62R Jan Staples, 86L Adrian Thomas, 92R Adrian Thomas, 111B Adrian Thomas, 120R A-Z, 121L Ron Bosser, 121R Mrs Monks, 139L Dan Sams; Ardea 18/9T Bob Gibbons, 21 Bob Gibbons, 56, 57L John Mason, 58R Peter Steyn, 66M John Clegg, 78 Bob Gibbons, 88 Ardea, 99 Ian Beames, 134 Bob Gibbons, 151LM Ardea; Jonathan Buckley 5, 6/7B, 13L, 13M, 13R, 14L, 14M, 15, 29, 37B, 42, 46/7B, 55, 58L, 82, 85L, 87R, 88R, 89L, 89R, 96, 115L, 115M, 117T, 120L, 120RM, 126, 128/9T, 141T,

146R, 149T, 150L, 153; Collections 22/3 Robin Weaver, 50/1 Robin Weaver, 103 Robert Estall, 106/7 Gary Smith, 136 Angela Hampton; Emap Publishing/ RHS 10 Tim Sandall; Garden Picture Library 31L Brian Carter, 14R J S Sira, 17 Howard Rice, 25 Jerry Pavia, 26 Clive Nichols, 27 Alec Scaresbrook, 31R David England, 32L John Glover, 32M Juliette Wade, 35M Brian Carter, 35R John Glover, 37T Howard Rice, 37M Juliette Wade, 38L Neil Homes, 38M Chris Burrows, 38R John Glover, 39L J S Sira, 39M Ron Evans, 39R Ron Sutherland, 52 Clive Bournsell, 60L, 61R Howard Rice, 63L Sunniva Harte, 63R Howard Rice, 64L Lamontagne, 66L, 66R, 67L Howard Rice, 73 John Glover, 74/5 Henk Oijkman, 86R Eric Crichton, 87L John Glover, 90L J S Sira, 90M John Glover, 90B Kit Young, 92L Ron Evans, 92M Geoff Dan, 93M Michel Viard, 93R Eric Crichton, 100/1T Michael Diggin, 100/1B Juliette Greene, 105 Gary Rogers, 108 John Glover, 112T

Neil Holmes, 112M Mayer/Le Scanff, 112B Jerry Pavia, 115B Juliette Wade, 117M David Cavanagnard, 117B Howard Rice, 118M Jerry Pavia, 118B Ron Evans, 120LM J S Sira, 137 Mayer/Le Scanff, 139R Roger Hyam, 141B Steven Wooster, 142T J S Sira, 142B John Glover, 145T, 145B Howard Rice, 146L Rex Butcher, 146M Mark Bolton, 149M Howard Rice, 149B Francois de Heel, 150RM Clive Nicholas, 150R GPL, 151L Ron Evans, 156 David Askham; Robert Harding 45 Duncan Maxwell, 130/1 RH; Harpur Garden Library 77, 98, 118T, 151R; Michael Holland 111T; Image State 6/7T, 79; Andrew Lawson 69, 93L, 102, 121M, 125, 128/9B; NHPA 74/5 E A Janes; Clive Nichols 151RM; Photos Horticultural 57R, 60R, 61L, 62L, 64R, 65L, 65R, 67M, 67R, 85R, 88L, 88M, 138, 150LM; Red Cover 18/9B Hugh Palmer; Woodfall Wild Images 4, 46/7T, 48 David Woodfall.